A LIFE'S JOURNEY

CHOICE AND CIRCUMSTANCE

ROBERT FURMAGA

PRISTINE
PRESS AND MEDIA

A Life's Journey
Copyright © 2025 by Robert Furmaga

ISBN
978-1-964804-37-8 (Paperback)
978-1-964804-36-1 (eBook)
978-1-964804-38-5 (Hardback)

A LIFE'S JOURNEY

CHOICE AND CIRCUMSTANCE

ROBERT FURMAGA

TABLE OF CONTENTS

Part 3 Persons of Interest

INTRODUCTION

In June 2022, I found myself in Houston, reconnecting with a friend I hadn't seen in over thirty years. I remembered the long summer of 1991 in New Orleans when he'd stayed with me while I toiled on a deepwater platform in the Gulf. Back then, his life was raw and uncertain; today, he navigates the oil and gas industry with the practiced ease of a seasoned consultant—his success evident in the warm glow of his home, the easy charm of his wife, and even the gleam of his small airplane.

During a late afternoon lunch, the subtle sizzle of steaks and the tang of a crisp salad mingled with the aroma of fine wine and freshly cut cigars. Between bites and quiet laughter, he leaned forward, his eyes soft yet insistent. "You should write about your journey," he urged. Inspired by his faith in me, I began to weave together a tapestry of fifty episodes spanning eighty-five years—a collection of memories that told the story of who I am.

I started with moments both tender and turbulent. I recalled my early defiance: the determined kicking and crying at nap time, my tiny being meeting my father's frustrated sternness. I still remember one chaotic afternoon as a child, when I clumsily managed to turn on a bathroom faucet and—unable to stop the stream—I darted down a sunlit street, bare as the truth, in desperate search of my father for help. Those vivid snapshots, as if captured in slow motion, have always been my secret treasure.

Even as a child, my mind seemed to store life in high-definition detail. Yet, while memories danced in crystal clarity, school smudged into a blur of distraction—until I discovered the saxophone. In private lessons, each soulful note brought focus and wonder, gradually transforming my scattered attention into a determination that led to a degree in engineering, earned at twenty-seven.

My career unfolded like a well-plotted adventure. I found myself solving problems on deepwater platforms one day and negotiating with senior executives the next. I met people who believed in doing things right and others whose ambition eroded basic decency. I'll never forget a conversation in a boardroom where one executive coldly justified letting loyal employees go just to fund a cosmetic touch-up for his plane. Yet, every time I encountered such imbalance, I also discovered genuine mentorship—a quiet nod, a shared joke, or an unexpected pat on the back that affirmed my own values.

In those moments, the factory hum of machines and the clatter of office chatter receded into a background that allowed personal connections to shine through. I realized then that every solution I engineered wasn't merely about fixing equipment, but about mending and nurturing relationships, too. Over the years, I learned that mentoring was not just a duty but a quiet gift—an ever-evolving conversation between hearts and minds.

Looking back, I also recognize a subtle pattern throughout my life: a tendency to slip away from discomfort, a penchant for retreating into memories or daydreams when faced with unwelcome truths. It's a trait that has both saved me and left its own mark on my story.

The chapters that follow trace this journey further. In "The Early Years," I explore how childhood misadventures and small victories set me on an unlikely path to engineering. "Career and Midlife" captures those long days of problem-solving—moments shared with colleagues who became teachers in more ways than one. In "Persons of Interest," I introduce the colorful characters who influenced my life, each etched with humor, integrity, or the scars of their early lives. "The Family" turns inward, chronicling the deep-rooted bonds that shaped my earliest sense of home. And finally, an addendum brings it all together with reflections gathered over decades—an update at 86, final thoughts on the winding road, and a meditation on the value of every stumble along the way.

A note for the curious reader: many of the business names and events in "Career and Midlife" dating back forty years are pseudonyms. In that era, companies like Zero Systems, Petro-xyz, CAC, AH, and NOC weren't just labels—they were entire worlds, now faded into memory as the landscape of industry has since transformed.

Even as I share these stories, I sense the faint stir of future chapters— silent promises of more revelations, unexpected turns, and the quiet echo of lessons yet to be learned.

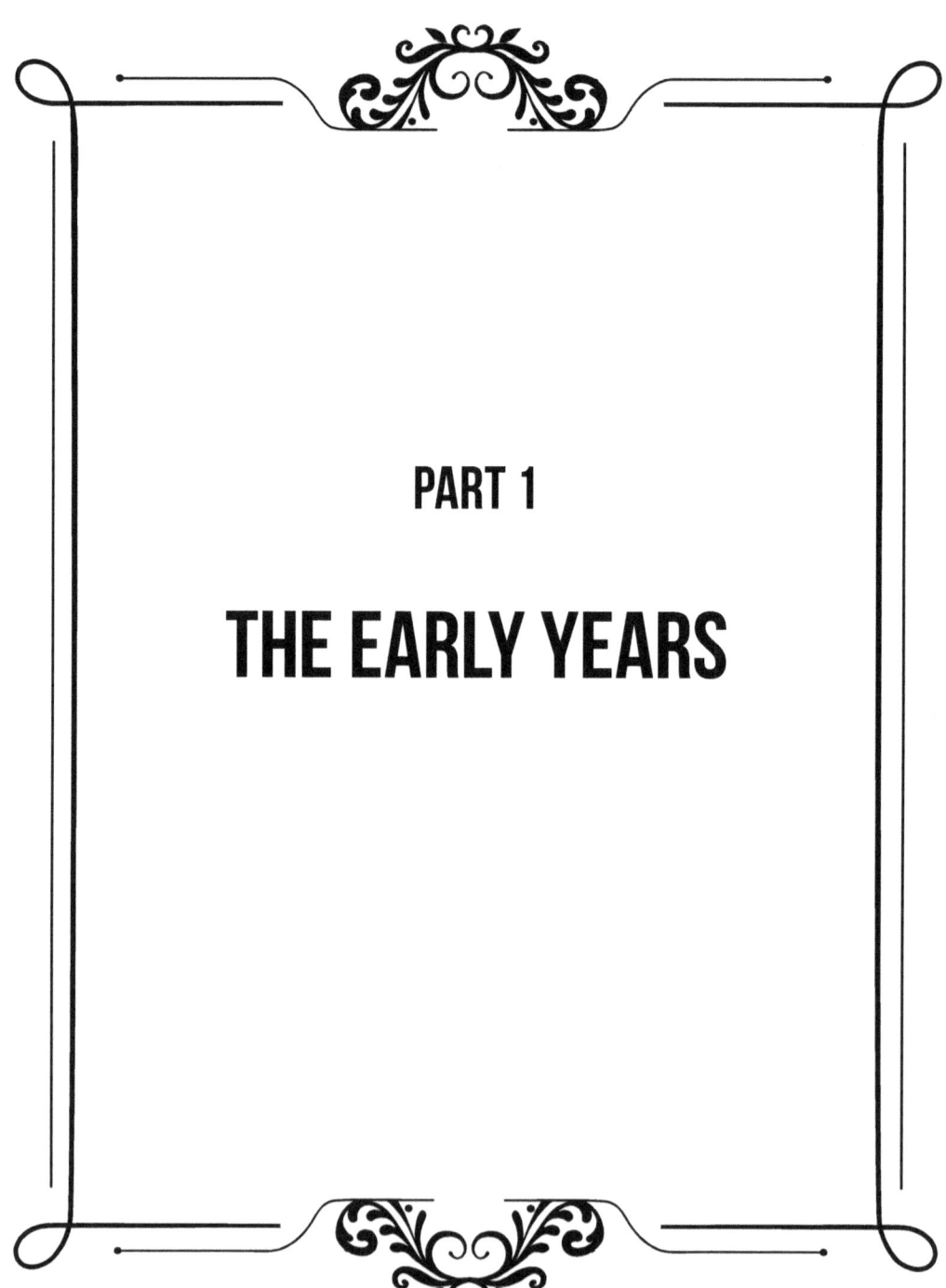

PART 1

THE EARLY YEARS

OUR HOME ON JULIAN

I still recall the warm haze of my earliest memories on Julian Street. One afternoon, my father was painting our front bedroom with freshly mixed peach linseed oil paint. I—barely three—hovered close, transfixed by the glimmer of wet color. "Don't touch the wall," he warned in a tone that left no room for argument. Of course, my little hand betrayed me. The instant I pressed my finger against that vibrant surface, the cool paint spread over my skin. My father's brush paused mid-stroke as he swatted my hand and wiped it clean with a rag steeped in turpentine. That small, charged moment quietly set the stage for a lifetime of cautious exploration and careful risk-taking.

I also remember quieter days, sprawled on the varnished wooden floor of our living room. I played with colorful letter blocks and a trusty spinning top, absorbing the gentle rhythm of family life. My mother's soft crocheted lace embellished a worn sofa while a floor radio glowed by the doorway—a backdrop to whispers and secret observations from my favorite hiding nooks in the buffet's side compartments.

In the kitchen, robust aromas signaled a new daily ritual. My mother orchestrated meals with the clatter of pans and laughter, while the room's simple charm—weathered linoleum and a modest wooden table—became a stage for our small dramas. Downstairs in the cool basement, the steady glow of a single light and the scratch of a broom on concrete grounded me in the tangible world of family labor and care. I watched as Mom balanced practical magic with everyday chores, setting the rhythm for the long winters warmed by the flickering dance of our coal furnace.

Nights brought their own kind of wonder and mischief. In our cramped bathroom, the ritual of bathtime with Lifebuoy left dark rings on porcelain, and in the gentle shadows I often hid behind the tub, mastering the art of quiet observation. Later, sleeping in a full-size bed with my sister, onetime turned into a midnight tumble under the bed—a scrambling search in the dark until Dad's light returned, banishing the cold and the fear.

The upstairs attic, with its bare wooden planks and icy windows, became our secret hideaway. My brothers and I—dubbed "the fire chiefs" by Dad when we exchanged wet pranks—shared whispered confessions under a single pull-string light. Wally, ever the contrarian, constructed model airplanes from nothing more than sticks and sheer determination. One summer, his dramatic display of setting his handmade Stuka dive bomber ablaze hinted at a future filled with rebellions and bold final acts.

Easter brought a living duck that quickly transformed from a pet to a somber meal—a memory that still echoes whenever I pass a quiet yard. I spent countless afternoons digging in the dirt near our back door, where pill bugs and centipedes were as real and welcome as any friend. The loss of our two parakeets, marked by a small funeral in a mason jar buried by a fence post, sealed the taste of life's fragile, fleeting moments.

Mondays and Thursdays carried us to the Hollywood Theatre on Fort Street, where a kindly ticket taker named Tom always welcomed us with a smile. Though I wasn't allowed in the main auditorium, I treasured the separate room where glass windows broadcast the magic of cinema to little eyes. After the film, we'd drift over to Senate Coney Island for hot dogs and root beer—a simple pleasure that lingered like the memory of that first carousel ride on Livernois Avenue. The bright lights, painted horses, and the soft hum of the ride became symbols of endless, carefree summers.

Family visits punctuated our lives with colorful stories. Trips to Aunt Clara and Uncle Frank's were filled with Sunday picnics at Belle Isle Park, where my mother's homemade treats and the scent of charcoal grills blended with the sound of raucous laughter. I still chuckle recalling how Dad and Uncle Frank, in a moment of unexpected abandon one Sunday afternoon, ended up in a minor altercation with the law over soaked shorts—a misadventure that, even then, hinted at the unpredictable tapestry of our shared history. A child's doctor set at Christmas, with its wooden instruments, was a cherished token of dreams too big for my small hands.

I also remember the thrill of riding my scooter on Joy Road, the wind whipping past as I navigated familiar corners and even dodged the mischief in a rat-infested garage near Livernois. When Dad took the car for repairs or to pick up parts on Warren Avenue, I sat in the back seat, my mind racing with excitement and wonder at the world unfolding around me. Even visits to Dr. Whitby—a kindly, jovial black dentist who helped me dodge more than just cavities—wove themselves into the fabric of my days.

MY FIRST VISIT TO CHICAGO

In the cool fall of 1940, my parents journeyed to Chicago to see Great-Aunt Mary. I still recall the coffee being made in her old glass percolator. In the dim pre-dawn light, a dropped egg mingled with the aroma of freshly brewed coffee—a scent that, though I was too young for the bitter taste, filled the room with quiet comfort. Aunt Mary's dining room, with its plastic fruit on the table and a gentle admonition— "Don't try eating that"—offered a glimpse into another kind of family warmth. Cousin Johnny's familiar greeting of "Little Bobby" sealed a bond that, even when years later the name sparked laughter and fond remembrance, never lost its sincere charm.

LIFE ON JULIAN

In our home on Julian, life was a study in contrasts. My parents, Walter and Sylvia, married on Valentine's Day in 1929, ushered in a world where strict discipline and tender care coexisted as our lives evolved. Wally, born February 1, 1930, by his teens, was skipping school and stealing, his character marked by moments of dishonesty. Gerry, born November 10, 1931, defied authority, grew stubborn and endured the harsh discipline as he perused his idea of sainthood. Rosemary, born January 4, 1933, felt every harsh word deeply, sometimes to tears as she was to become self-complacent and a "tell-all.' I arrived unplanned on June 5, 1937, became the silent observer, absorbing family experiences and quiet stories, some too delicate to be spoken.

In those early years, while Dad's belt set the unyielding rules, I learned to slip into the quiet corners of our bustling household. Even as discipline loomed large, the light of small rebellions, secret hideaways, and quiet laughter promised that every harsh lesson was also the seed of future understanding—a subtle foreshadowing of the winding, transformative path that lay ahead.

WWII

For me, it all began on a crackling Sunday afternoon when the radio filled the room with urgency. I sat wide-eyed as my family hurried about—my older siblings absorbed the news while I tried to understand the commotion. Days later my father proudly accepted his naturalized citizenship—a secret victory for him after years of claiming he'd been born in the middle of the ocean—I sensed change stirring beneath familiar routines.

Evenings took us past glowing factories and the bright lights of the Lincoln Motor Plant on Livernois Avenue. I remember the summer air carrying sparks from grinder work through open windows. By late 1942, Uncle Frank, behind the wheel of his 1939 Dodge Coupe, would navigate the Detroit-Windsor Tunnel on Saturdays to fetch meat and other rationed goods. I can still taste the sweet tang of Canadian bacon—the kind that promised respite from harsh realities.

In 1943, Uncle Frank's draft into the Marines left his favorite necktie draped over the dining-room chair until his return, a silent reminder of absent heroes. War-themed radio shows and soap operas painted our evenings with headlines and heroic tales. I clutched a secret coding ring and a paper airbase I had ordered by mailing in little treasures like box tops and quarters, checking the mailbox every afternoon until the package finally arrived, slow as a drawn-out promise.

Schooldays blurred together with scavenged paper and flattened tin cans, while our victory garden and war stamps were our small rebellions against a world in turmoil. At home, the Cunningham News Ace broke in and out with updates, and Dad—working part-time for a used-car dealer, repaired cars with no parts and a cutting tool that made tires look new. Even as gas grew scarce, and a race riot erupted, our everyday struggles and life in our neighborhood retained a curious purity—a quiet, unspoken respect that prevailed despite everything.

Before the war truly loomed, our neighbor Mr. Washburn ran a cozy bird-feed store on Warren Avenue. Saturday evenings were alight with the flicker of his rented Hollywood films from the '30s. I remember his projector's beam dancing against the wall, as Rosemary practically begged, "Can we join you?" With no children of their own, Mr. Washburn and his wife welcomed us, and soon our ragtag band of kids cleared a vacant lot next door to transform it into our own outdoor theater. We worked together under the warm glow of a late summer sun, our laughter mingling with the scent of freshly cut grass and Mrs. Washburn's homemade cookies and milk—a taste of pure, simple joy amid wartime uncertainty.

Then there was Roberta Taylor, who lived just across the alley. I'd catch glimpses of her as she left for school with Rosemary, but one evening changed everything. After washing dishes on a chair in our bustling kitchen, a soft voice called, "Bobby, come here!" I followed, and Roberta tugged my hand beneath the open sink where a towel served as our secret curtain. She leaned in and pressed a gentle kiss to my lips—a moment so fleeting and innocent that it broke into giggles when Rosemary burst through the door. Even years later, that quiet, daring spark of first affection lingered in my memory.

By 1944, as a seven-year-old riding the milk route with Dad, time itself seemed to quicken. On Saturday nights, mischief came in unexpected packages. I remember when Wally and his friends discovered their own brand of entertainment—squeezing into our darkened bathroom to catch a glimpse of Joey, our neighbor in her early twenties. Their whispered excitement soon turned to panic when Rosemary, ever vigilant, flung open the door with a shocked, "What's going on here?" Amid frantic orders to "turn off the light," the impromptu voyeurism ended as swiftly as it had begun. That night, the bathroom's glow faded along with the boys' secret adventure, leaving behind only the memory of juvenile curiosity and its inevitable consequences.

Each of these moments—the radio's hum of change, the bittersweet taste of rationed treats, the thrill of a forbidden first kiss, and the awkward adventures of youth—wove together into the tapestry of my early years, hinting at the unexpected turns that would shape my life long after the echoes of war had faded.

ST. LUKE'S: STARTING SCHOOL

I longed to join my neighborhood friends at Sherrill Elementary, but my Catholic parents had different plans. Instead, I set off for St. Luke's—a long, weather-beaten mile that took me across busy streets, quiet backyards, and even railroad tracks. I spent another year at home helping Mom before finally stepping into first grade after my sixth birthday.

Despite a knack for remembering details, reading was a puzzle. Sunday mornings, I sat by the window, eyes fixed on Detroit Times comics while Uncle Don's warm radio voice brought them to life. I still recall the shock when, one day, he ended his show with a careless, "Well, that takes care of the little bastards for another week." His final words echoed in my head long after those mornings faded.

First grade passed in a haze of tests I could not conquer. Then came second grade and Sister Beatrice—a tiny, determined woman in a heavy black habit whose booming commands left little room for error. "Come here. Hold out your hand," she'd snap, and a thick, oversized ruler would quickly follow. I watched the colorful star chart on the wall fill with names and symbols while mine lingered with barely two stars. One afternoon, she handed out a drawings of sinners burning in hell for us to color. I filled in my picture with bright reds, yellows, and a hint of orange, wondering why I never earned a better grade.

Learning cursive was a messy affair too. Black ink stained my small fingers as I struggled to form neat loops, and even raising my hand to ask for a break sometimes ended in chaos—a memory marked by Maureen Connolly's desperate fidgeting until she finally let nature take its course.

Preparing for my First Communion thrust me into a world of mortal sins, confession, and penance. I prayed earnest, wanting to get to heaven. After confession, I asked God to take me now, this was going to be tough. No luck, I would have to endure my imperfections. After school in winter, I bundled into layers of leggings, galoshes, a heavy coat, scarf, cap, and gloves for the long walk home. Mornings were especially nerve-wracking, crossing the railroad tracks near Tireman Avenue while trains rumbled to life. I remember placing pennies on the rails, watching them flatten under roaring engines, and imagining the war production from the Ford plant in the trailing freights cars. In spring, puddles formed by the tracks brimmed with tadpoles and tiny turtles. By the time I reached home, burrs clung stubbornly to my socks—a small, constant reminder of each day's adventure.

June somehow ushered in a promotion to third grade, and by the fall of 1945, as new houses rose near the tracks on Central Avenue, my friend Carl and I turned a deep drainage ditch into our personal obstacle course. One reckless tug on my shirt sent me tumbling into the ditch—my scream and rushed steps echoing as I called out for Dad, clutching my broken left arm. The shock of that fall would haunt me as I nursed a displaced fracture, only to test fate again on icy winter paths.

A visit to Dr. Edwin Watson—ushered in by a gentle, kind nurse—proved a turning point. I don't recall much of the exchange, but as Dr. Watson led me out, he firmly told my mother, "Get him out of there!" That brusque command, as unsettling as it was, felt like a promise that salvation might yet be found in unexpected places.

After finishing third grade at St. Luke's, I transferred to Sherrill. Struggling with reading and memorization, I sought solace in art, science, gym, shop, and music—areas where my fingers and eyes could learn on their own. Comic books and newspapers became my tutors, and gradually, classics like Paddle-to-the-Sea and Sherlock Holmes filled in my growing love for stories. I even started playing the C-melody saxophone, its tentative notes hinting at new possibilities that private music lessons would later unlock.

Yet, one task remained unfinished: Confirmation. For months, I attended after-school catechism on Tuesdays and Thursdays—a steady, insistent ritual of prayers and lessons that eventually carried me over the threshold of understanding. Little did I know, these early trials and the steady rhythm of daily walks, harsh teachers, and small acts of rebellion were quietly setting the stage for the person I was destined to become.

ON TO SHERRILL

Salvation felt real the moment I stepped through the doors of Sherrill Elementary. My new world burst to life in Mrs. Williams's science classroom, where a quirky mix of pith helmets, tan shorts, and a gleaming postwar brown Jeep set the tone for discovery. Insects and glass cases revealed secret worlds—a Polyphemus moth here, a praying mantis there—and even the humble transformation of a neighbor's plump caterpillar into a butterfly seemed nothing short of miraculous. Warm autumn days were spent chasing grasshoppers until their "tobacco juice" splattered on my skin, or trudging through weed-choked fields only to find burrs clinging stubbornly to my socks.

Gym class under Mr. Drinkwater was its own kind of adventure. With a smile and a booming voice, he led us through kickball, dodgeball, and even square dancing to records from a bygone era. In art, we splashed bright colors on papier-mâché figures and experimented with copper stencils, while music and math came naturally—leaving reading and spelling as challenges to overcome with quiet determination.

As the years passed, fifth, sixth, and seventh grades blurred into a continuous thrill of new skills and secret mischief. I took shop class, learned to play the saxophone, and built up my vocabulary under the patient tutelage of Mrs. Shaw. Evenings and weekends became a time for rebellion and camaraderie: racing home to catch radio serials like The Lone Ranger, playing rubber gun war games, and sharing stolen moments of streetwise "education" with my neighborhood friends.

Saturday matinees at the Annex Theatre on Grand River Avenue grew into a cherished ritual. We'd huddle in front of flickering screens as cartoons gave way to eerie crime and horror films—Bela Lugosi, Boris Karloff, and even a surprise appearance by a live magician setting our imaginations alight. Afterwards, our escapades continued on a scavenger's quest at Kresge's, sometimes daring to pocket a small toy as our mischievous trophy.

School wasn't always fun, though. Volunteering for the Safety Patrol in sixth grade seemed like a shortcut to freedom until its bitter side revealed itself. One chilly afternoon I pleaded, "Mrs. Hutchins, I don't want to be on the Safety Patrol anymore." Her flat reply, "There's no one to replace you. You can't quit," was followed by a playground vendetta from a classmate, Wally Kent, that ended with the assistant principal storming in. With one sharp slap and a yank of my Safety Patrol belt, she declared, "You don't belong on the Safety Patrol." Stinging cheek pressed against the classroom desk, I secretly cheered at my relief—even as I braced for a father's lecture that never came. Instead, a quiet "Hi, Dad!" accompanied my escape back to the familiar laughter of friends and an unexpected "U" in Auditorium marking my exit.

Yet, Sherrill was more than a collection of classroom mishaps and minor rebellions. It was a time of endless adventure. On lazy summer afternoons off my father's schedule, my friends and I strolled the railroad tracks from Livernois to Oakwood Boulevard near the Beverly Theater, our laughter mingling with the distant rumble of trains. Other days found us sneaking a swim at Mackenzie High School's indoor pool before ending the day with Dairy Queen cones on Joy Road—sweet treats that hinted at a fast food world just beginning to open.

We filled our days with softball, baseball, and the wild exploits of The Night Raiders—a gang that turned vacant lots into playgrounds and alleys into secret orchards where we plucked apples and plums until the sun dipped below the horizon. In winter, I shoveled snow with determined grit; in summer, I trimmed lawns with a push mower to earn a little extra cash. As I grew older, I joined my brother Wally on increasingly daring ventures, each adventure a quiet rehearsal for what lay ahead.

Then, in 1950, life shifted again. A move led to my eighth grade at Cerveny Middle School under Mrs. Murphy—a formidable presence whose booming threats ("If you don't be quiet, I'm going to land on you!") were as memorable as they were intimidating. Surviving that turbulent year paved my way to Cooley High School—a milestone that felt like the culmination of every small victory at Sherrill.

A defining moment arrived when I had to choose between a general program and a college-preparatory track. In a hushed classroom, as Mrs. Murphy called each name, I declared with a mix of nerves and bravado, "College prep!" Her burst of laughter—equal parts disbelief and amusement—echoed in the room. I later suspected that shared chuckles in the teachers' lounge carried the rumor of my bold ambition. Even as I recalled the mirth in her eyes, I knew that every laugh, every misadventure, and every challenge at Sherrill was quietly steering me toward a future I was just beginning to imagine.

THE WILD RIDE

Two years after we left the old neighborhood and just finishing ninth grade, a bright Michigan summer morning in 1952 promised nothing more than a nostalgic walk through memories. I caught the Six-Mile Road bus, switched to the Livernois bus, and finally stepped off at Joy Road. Strolling those familiar streets, the past seemed close when a battered Chevy sedan skidded to a halt before me. Inside, Loren, Jerry, and Bill—all familiar gang members from my youth—grinned with reckless invitation.

"Hey, Bob! Jump in, let's go for a ride," Loren called with a wild gleam in his eyes.

The moment I clambered into the car, Loren's joyride began. Only fifteen and granted a driver's license through parental favors, he treated the open road like his personal racetrack. He tore along residential lanes at breakneck speeds, swerving over curbs without a care. I shifted uncomfortably in my seat, watching the world blur outside as my pulse pounded in protest.

As we neared Livernois, I seized my escape. "Let me out at the corner—I need to catch the bus," I said, voice trembling with relief. With hurried goodbyes, I leaped onto the waiting bus, heart still racing from the wild, untamed ride.

A few days later, a headline in the morning paper nearly made my stomach drop. Loren had been speeding the previous night, darting away from a threat—or so he claimed. But on a sharp turn on Outer Drive, he lost control. The Chevy slammed into a tree, and Jerry, unrestrained in the passenger seat, was flung through the windshield, killed on impact. I lingered over the words, wondering if Loren had truly been chased or if the story was a desperate fabrication to escape a manslaughter charge.

That tight-knit crew had once spent countless hours playing baseball on the school diamond, with Jerry always at the heart of it—a catcher with a confident grin, signaling plays like a pro. Now, that familiar image was burned into my mind as a forever lost moment. Memories of after-school games, wild adventures, and even crude jokes filled in the gaps of a time when we believed nothing mattered, yet the sudden loss made clear that nothing stayed the same.

I never saw those old friends again. Sometimes, I'd catch a glimpse of a faded smile or a familiar nickname, small echoes of a misfit youth both cherished and flawed.

Life had always danced dangerously close to disaster for me. I recalled narrowly avoiding a speeding car in the alley behind the grocery store and the day I clutched the edge of a boat in Orchard Lake, refusing to let go until I reached safety. Eventually, I learned to swim at the YMCA, perhaps out of necessity as much as defiance. Later, air travel, highway driving, and my work in the petroleum industry only deepened my understanding that risk was an ever-present companion.

Irony, however, had its cruel sense of humor. My friend A.J.—a safety engineer who spent his days preaching caution and installing signs—was tragically crushed by a reversing dump truck in his own front yard. The twist was as bitter as it was inexplicable.

In those moments, I often wondered what fate had in store. Would it be a senseless act of envy, an unforeseen accident, or simply the gradual unraveling of life behind sterile walls? Despite all the calculated risks and careful maneuvers, fate remained elusive—a promise only time could reveal.

RUTH

It was a crisp September morning as I strolled along Fenkell Avenue, carrying my saxophone on my way to Cooley High. That day, a Chevy screeched to a stop, and the window rolled down to reveal Mr. Warner Weiss. He asked, "Would you be interested in private saxophone lessons?" His unexpected offer set me on a path that, over the next four years, saw me mastering both saxophone and clarinet—eventually earning a music scholarship to Wayne State University.

In tenth grade, my world shifted the moment I met Ruth. A gifted piano player and daughter of a professional cornetist, she carried herself with a mix of confidence and quiet passion. We clicked instantly. One afternoon, with a spark in her eyes, she proposed we start a band. Soon, Ronnie's trumpet, Don's steady drumbeats, and Tom's trombone joined our ragtag ensemble. At first, we called ourselves "The Four Cats and a Kitten," but after a year of practice and a few Friday-night school dances, "The Hi-Fi's" emerged as our new name.

Our friendship deepened during junior and senior years. We spent evenings at movies, shared hayrides, and danced under string lights at school functions. Yet, even as we navigated the tangled thrill of first love, complications arose. One chilly evening before senior prom, I hesitantly asked, "Ruth, will you be my date?" She paused, her voice soft and conflicted, "Jack asked me too—I haven't decided." Weeks later, when she finally chose Jack, the disappointment hit me hard, but I needed a date.

Not long after, Judy—a bright, quick-witted junior from my trigonometry class—stepped into the void. We were friends, joked in class and secretly planned for the prom. On that unforgettable night, as I picked her up and admired the way the dim streetlights caught her smile, we casually sidled up behind Ruth and Jack. Ruth's stunned silence was met with a quiet introduction: "This is Judy." In retrospect, I sometimes wonder if my fixation on Ruth blinded me to what might have been with Judy.

Graduation came in a warm summer haze. Ruth departed for a music university in Ohio while I embarked on an engineering program.

For two years, our letters bridged the distance, and holiday breaks filled with shared laughter and lingering touches kept our connection alive.

Ruth was home on spring break and one evening, she invited me to a picnic at a secluded park off Fenkell near Telegraph Road. We spread a checkered blanket in a grassy clearing lit only by a single streetlight and the ember glow of fading coals from the grill. The mild, still air wrapped around us as we lay side by side beneath clusters of maple trees. I could still see the vivid strands of her fiery red hair dancing around her gentle face. In the hushed night, as I traced the curve of her lips with a tentative kiss, all my youthful doubts vanished—leaving behind a feeling of unguarded honesty, fragile and eternal.

In those tender moments, I was completely taken over by a deeper love for her. Ruth had captured my very soul. Yet as we neared nineteen, the intimacy of our connection matured into something more complex. The distance between us widened along with the divergence of our dreams. A misunderstanding later exploded into a painful breakup, a wound that would transform the way I approached love. From that day on, I began to build walls around my heart, measuring risk with cautious calculation.

Even now, the memory of those reckless rides, shared romantic secrets, and those tender, isolated moments in the park serves as both a reminder of my first true love and a foreshadowing of the guarded years that followed.

THE FREE PRESS

Late April's heat was already bearing down as graduation loomed, and I felt the pressure of my probationary music scholarship to Wayne State slip through the cracks of my weak college prep grades. Trigonometry and English composition—two subjects I dreaded failing—kept me up at night.

I remember pleading with Mr. Twitchell, my gentle, aging trigonometry teacher. "Mr. Twitchell, I really need a passing grade," I said, desperation mingling with a hint of rebellion. "I have a music scholarship—can you at least give me a D?" I didn't expect that grade to matter later, but it did. Years afterward, I would learn that life had dealt him a harsh hand too—he'd been forced into retirement and eventually taken his own life.

Mr. Niblett was another mountain to climb. His red pen sliced through every essay I wrote, his critiques hinging on the way my letters merged on the page. Every piece of handwritten work of mine was reduced to a D or "fail," and with each mark, my future seemed more uncertain.

At the start of the senior year, I finally broke free from my father's milk route. "Dad, five dollars a week isn't enough," I argued one fall morning, stepping away from that familiar task. I soon landed a job as an usher at the Great Lakes Theatre—a grueling two-mile walk in the dead of winter after midnight shows, but one that gave me a taste of independence.

In early May, my father sold me his 1948 Pontiac for a mere sixty dollars. With the car and a word from Uncle Phil—who worked as a truck driver at the Detroit Free Press—I decided to apply for a job in the Circulation Department. I still remember stepping out of a second-floor elevator and, on a whim, turning right when I saw the "Circulation" sign, only to find myself in the Display Advertising office.

"Can I help you?" asked Bob Brant at the counter.

"I'm looking for a job in Circulation," I replied, not grasping the possibilities.

He grinned, introduced me to Mr. Armstrong, and within minutes I was hired as a messenger. My schedule—3:00 to 8:00 p.m. five days a week—was tailor-made for a student juggling school and work. Later, when Saturdays were added, my workload climbed to thirty-three hours a week, but it was a sacrifice for my future. That summer, I even studied music with a member of the Detroit Symphony while registering for classes at Wayne State.

I sometimes think back to Bob Brant—a kid who finished high school at fourteen, so small and out of place in college that he soon retreated into alcohol before finding odd work at the Free Press. His brief presence in that corridor taught me that every path has its forks.

I had once dreamt of attending Ford Trade School, but when it closed, doubts about a music career crept in. One day, I confided my worries to our next-door neighbor, Mrs. Larson, who had once crammed tenth-grade algebra into three evenings with me. Though my grades didn't soar overnight, I began to grasp math in ways that could matter. Encouraged by her, I took an eight-hour aptitude test from the Detroit Board of Education in early August. When the advisor mentioned architectural engineering and journalism—fields I'd never even considered—it shifted the landscape of my future.

With time running short, I applied to Lawrence Tech for engineering. I still recall sitting in the dean's office as he skimmed over my lackluster high school record—except for the shining A's in music. Then he looked up, his tone unexpectedly kind. "You scored exceptionally high on the admission test. You can register for the architecture program right away." It was a turning point I hadn't seen coming.

A year and a half later, as the night clerk at the paper was departing, I spotted my opportunity. "Can I take over?" I asked Mr. Armstrong without missing a beat. "It's yours," he said. And so I became the night clerk—working from 8:00 p.m. to 1:00 a.m., a quiet job of studying, then walking over to collect advertising engravings and mats from the Detroit News and Detroit Times, pieces that went into assembling the next day's papers. My first year on the desk felt like a well-oiled machine.

The following summer brought challenges of its own. Ken Kramer, a daytime colleague from advertising, needed to swap shifts to attend class. I agreed, only to have my routine upended when he convinced Mr. Armstrong that the late shifts weren't necessary, stripping away my precious study time. By fall, my new schedule stretched from 4:30 to 10:30 p.m. Monday through Friday, plus 8:00 a.m. to 5:00 p.m. on Saturdays. Exhausted but resolute, I kept going, clinging to the belief I could manage the hardship, overcoming new obstacles.

LAWRENCE TECHNOLOGICAL UNIVERSITY

In the crisp fall of 1955, I arrived at Lawrence Tech with my slide rule swinging from my belt—a modest talisman as I faced the challenge ahead. The aptitude test was a blur of series equations I'd never seen, yet math never let me down. Even with an 18-credit schedule and long nights at the Free Press, I managed a surprising 90 percent on analytical geometry test by simply skimming sample problems.

By my second year, I fell into classical physics and calculus—disciplines that quietly steered me toward electrical engineering. I dove into mechanics courses—statics, dynamics, fluid mechanics—while my nights at the Free Press left me scrambling to make morning classes. In junior year, thermodynamics with Hans Ernemann, the stern dean of mechanical engineering, became my crucible. Ernemann would launch each morning lecture with a snippet of his life in Germany. I struggled to be on time, often slipping in well after 8:00 a.m. The final, an open-book exam, focused on superheated steam calculations, I nailed it! Instead, Ernemann slammed down my paper, accusing me of cheating, and handed me a D. I suspected his harsh grade was less about the test and more about my chronic lateness. No more courses with Hans!

Exams during my junior and senior years often averaged in the forties and fifties. In my statics class, a full slate of eager students dwindled to a handful by midterm, and my rank swayed with every withdrawal. Professor Levenson's steady, honest grading eventually earned me a hard-won C—a small victory in a system that felt designed to break you.

The weight of 18-credit semesters—12 being the minimum for my student draft deferment—gradually wore me down. My GPA slipped; I dropped and even failed a few classes. The late nights eventually blurred into long days, and I found myself turning to the bottle to dull the relentless pressure. I continued paying room and board to my father, who was struggling to keep up with the financial demands of our new Norfolk Avenue home, a burden compounded by my brother Gerry's youthful indiscretions. Even as most of my engineering courses proceeded without a hitch, advanced AC circuit classes left me scrambling. I had two warnings letters from the draft board, and I was beginning to unravel.

Yet, amid the chaos of equations and deadlines, unexpected kindness offered moments of respite. In 1957, shortly after our move to Norfolk Avenue, I met Hyman Shankman—a neighbor whose gentle manner belied the hardships of a Polish immigrant raising two children on his own drapery business. Every winter, his old Dodge sputtered to life with a push from me at dawn. "There you go, Bob," he'd say, his accented voice warm against the chill. His steady presence was a small anchor. In 1964, when I finally graduated, Hyman handed me a beautiful leather case—a silent token of care that I carried with me through the trials of my engineering career.

Those years at Lawrence Tech were a tumult of late-night study sessions, unexpected grades that cut deep, and the constant balancing act between passion and survival. I learned that even when the academic world seems cold and unforgiving, a neighbor's kind words or a small gift can be the spark that keeps you moving forward. And sometimes, in the midst of unraveling plans and mounting risks, it's those moments of genuine connection that quietly set you back on course.

SAM

It all began with my nightly walks to the Detroit News—sometimes the Times—to collect engravings and mats for the next day's ads. Mr. Armstrong would put the final touches on the page layouts before 5:00 p.m., sending them off to the composing room where "printer's devils" merged Linotype text with inked engravings. The finished pages were proofed and processed, destined for presses that churned them out to homes across the state.

Sam was in his early twenties at the News, working alongside Ed Nagel—a devoted family man—and Phil Brooks, slim and quiet, barely my age. I had known Sam for about a year when, fresh off my twenty-first birthday, he invited me to Frank's Bar for a bite. Friday nights became our escape: after finishing work around 10:30 p.m., I'd meet Sam at Frank's, where bartender Pete and the low hum of conversation set the stage for easy laughter and shared dreams.

In time, our Friday nights extended into Saturday escapades near Vernor and Junction—bowling, hot dogs, and beers that seemed to wash away the stress of classes. Yet not all was light. I watched, helpless, as Phil's nightly indulgence masked a silent battle; his casual drinking belied a secret—leukemia—that would claim him within three years.

As if fate weren't already unpredictable enough, Sam's life veered suddenly. He met a girl on a wild first date, and before long, she was pregnant. Four months later, under relentless pressure from his mother, he married her. I tried to warn him, "Sam, just pay support," but he plunged forward. The marriage, marred by another pregnancy and constant tension, unraveled after just five turbulent months, leaving him supporting his ex-wife and two children. With nowhere else to turn, he returned to our Friday nights at Frank's, though the sparkle in his eyes had long since faded.

My Saturdays grew busier, too. After my shift at the Free Press, I'd steal away to my brother-in-law Richard's for long, philosophical debates over a large bottle of Meister Brau. In the evenings, a quick shower and power nap would reset my mind before I met Sam at 9:00 p.m. to watch Paladin. Later, we'd hit the Times Square Bar, swapping stories with characters like Judy—a young woman caught in a downward spiral—or venture to the Lafayette Bar. Meanwhile, my own restless Sundays drifted between bowling at the Log Cabin with Sam, followed by tense rounds of liar's poker in the bar. The weight of it all was palpable: by December, I'd be joining the army for three years, and Sam would vanish to California, desperate to outrun his past.

Years later, Sam returned to Detroit. He found solace in Nancy—a warm, steady presence who shared his late-night bar scene and impromptu family trips to Traverse City. When I visited, I'd always drop by their apartment near the airport, where their quiet companionship shone brightly for nearly fifty years. But after Nancy suffered a sudden stroke and died shortly after, Sam's loneliness deepened. His sister Mary had passed two years earlier to lung cancer, and the few friends he had left drifted away. Even his favorite bar lost its charm, and eventually, the isolation and despair overwhelmed him, leading him to end his life with alcohol and barbiturates.

One damp Sunday night in early spring, I drove down Vernor Avenue and pulled into Mike's Place. Inside, the murmur of late-night conversation mingled with clinking glasses. I spotted Phil sitting at a table with two striking young women, and shortly after, I joined them. Tired eyes and quiet smiles passed between us as Phil introduced me to Marlene and Jackie. But before long, Phil announced he was done— "I've been with them all weekend. I'm done, I need some sleep"—and he slipped away.

Marlene and Jackie lingered, and I offered them a ride home. As we wound our way through the rain-slicked streets, Jackie leaned closer, and I sensed the spark of something new amid the night's quiet murmur. We pulled up to a modest house with a high porch. While Marlene fumbled for her keys in the dark, I stood next to Jackie. Then, heavy footsteps echoed. A large man seized my shoulder and spun me around, slamming me against the door. "What are you doing with my wife?" he demanded, voice rough with anger. Time froze. Before I could react, Marlene stepped in, her tone cool and commanding: "He's with me." The man released me, and I staggered back, my heart pounding in my ears.

I exchanged a few hushed words with Marlene, thanking her for intervening, and left soon after—shaken, but intact. That night, as I drove away under the sparse glow of streetlights, I vowed silently: never again would I pick up strangers without caution.

Every step of the journey—from late-night runs at the News to the bittersweet tang of lost friendships and precarious nights—reminded me that life is a wild ride, full of unexpected turns. And amid the chaos and fleeting laughter, moments of genuine connection could, for a brief while, anchor you before the next storm hit.

TIME FOR ANOTHER CAR

By the end of junior year, my 1949 Plymouth had finally run out of steam—like the weary horse in *Gone with the Wind*, it collapsed upon arrival. Fuel economy fell to a dismal forty miles per quart of 50-weight oil, and patching a hole in the muffler with a three-pound coffee tin became routine. I had a hole in the rear floorboard and rolling down the windows to escape choking exhaust was no way to face a Michigan winter, especially when gas cost just twenty cents a gallon and beer was a quarter a bottle.

One Sunday, browsing the classifieds, I spotted a 1955 DeSoto Firedome V8 Gray Club Coupe for $550. It looked like the perfect ride to carry me through graduation. With my dad cosigning a personal loan, I soon found myself gripping a new steering wheel and a future that seemed just a bit brighter.

But new wheels brought new troubles. On a frigid January night, I drove along Michigan Avenue at ten miles per hour on icy, snow-covered roads. I saw an Oldsmobile stop abruptly for a turn, its bumper jutting into my lane. I tried to stop, but the ice refused to cooperate, and I slid right under his bumper. The other car emerged unscathed while mine took a hard hit. I called the police, only to be ticketed. In court the referee warned, "Keep your mouth shut, or you'll convict yourself."

For a while, I navigated town with a damaged front end. Then one morning, as my car sat outside our Norfolk home, I watched a pickup truck, stuck in an icy rut, smash into my rear. I witnessed the whole scene from our picture window. The driver, initially poised to flee, eventually knocked on our door. His insurance covered the repairs, and soon enough I was back on the road—rusted rocker panels patched with fiberglass and repainted for a bargain at Earl Scheib's.

Around that time, Sam picked up a 1954 Packard Clipper hardtop, its brown and tan body gleaming with hefty whitewall tires. He was usually a confident, capable driver, but one New Year's Eve in Ecorse, something felt off. As we left a party for downtown Detroit via West Jefferson Avenue, Sam's erratic stops—slowing to a crawl at red lights then speeding off—made my pulse race. "Sam, want me to drive?" I finally asked. He said nothing, and after countless lights, we pulled up to Lafayette Coney Island for coffee and hot dogs. When I later mentioned his driving, he insisted he remembered nothing unusual.

GOODBYE COLETTE

While working at the Free Press, I dabbled in dating. I once spent afternoons with Linda Unthank—sharp and witty—visiting museums and catching plays at the Shakespeare Festival. Then Joey Nederlander, a familiar face at Display Advertising who would later manage major New York theatres, handed me tickets to *My Fair Lady* at the Riviera. I invited a charming woman from Windsor, and after the show we wandered into the Blue Bird Inn for outstanding jazz. I drove her home that night, but as life often does, it swept us apart without another word.

Autumn Saturdays at the Free Press became ritual. I'd head out for a pool game at the Old Detroit Recreation Building, then grab a corned beef sandwich and a cold beer from the bar across the street. A quick 25-cent shoeshine, a Dutch Master cigar on a pleasant day, and a stop at a Polish bakery on Michigan Avenue for dark pumpernickel—each little act was a quiet rebellion against the everyday grind. Back home, I'd whip up my own chili—a recipe that still warms me on cold nights.

By summer 1960, my degree seemed further away than ever. Weekends merged into nights of drinking with Sam, wrestling with existential philosophy, and confronting a stubborn depression. I even flirted with the idea of naval aviation—until a minor test derailed that path. Instead, I enrolled in a night course on gas turbine design and took mechanical vibrations in the fall. Then, in December, my draft notice arrived. At twenty-three, the weight of everything felt like the final collapse of a long-failing structure.

Somewhere amid the chaos, I met Colette—a tall, striking woman in her early twenties. We dated briefly, sharing quiet moments that hinted at something lasting. But one Sunday night, after a movie, I suddenly realized

I was in too deep. I left her apartment and never called again. I couldn't find the right words to explain or to even say, "Goodbye Colette."

ARMY YEARS

On December 2, my father drove me to the front gate of Fort Wayne for processing and induction. The day was overcast and chilly—around forty degrees—while I shuffled through endless paperwork and a physical exam punctuated by a crude command: "Bend over and spread your cheeks!" By afternoon, I'd done everything except the swearing-in. A clerk sent me to wait in a nearby building; I crept up, only to hear loud banging that sent me scurrying to the PX for coffee and pie. At the swearing-in, I noted the grimy faces of recruits, likely worn down by stacking bleachers.

That evening, I journeyed by train to Louisville and then a bus to Fort Knox, where I received my basic training uniform and supplies. Assigned to a wooden barrack set apart from the main post, I learned quickly that isolation was part of the package. A coal furnace in our two-story building needed constant stoking by the fire guard every few hours. If he dozed off, by 3:00 a.m., the cold would creep in. I'd assumed Kentucky winters would be kinder; reality proved otherwise.

A few weeks in, during KP duty, I witnessed a shipment of premium meat being siphoned off by the company sergeant, cooks, and a few NCOs. The sergeant's cautious rationing every morning hinted at unspoken corruption—reporting it was unthinkable, a surefire ticket down the barracks stairs.

Before the Army, I'd prided myself on impeccable hygiene—apart from the usual teenage acne. Yet military life introduced me to boils, spawned by seemingly pristine latrine seats harboring invisible bacteria. I endured multiple boils, one severe enough to land me in Fort Monmouth's hospital for a week. Eventually, I discovered that applying ethyl alcohol every few days helped keep the outbreaks at bay—a small, personal ritual that became my silent shield.

January and February at Fort Knox tested us to the limit. Nighttime obstacle courses under live gunfire were daunting; attempting them during the day on wet sand that froze into razor-sharp ice was nearly impossible. The next morning, when the sergeant called five men for a truck detail and I wasn't named, I slipped on anyway. I found a quiet corner at the supply warehouse, read a few magazines, and even grabbed a nap—a tiny victory in the relentless routine.

At twenty-three, I was older than most recruits—many just eighteen and oblivious to the looming specter of Vietnam. I was also twenty pounds overweight, but by late February, I'd shed the excess and molded myself into a soldier.

My first commercial flight, in late February, whisked me from Louisville to a New Jersey Army base amid falling snow. Soon after, I was in a microwave radio repair course at Fort Monmouth, where I met Ken Keitches, an NCO who quickly became my confidant. Fort Monmouth felt like a college campus, and I spent a magical summer in Asbury Park with Ken—cruising in his MG sports car and dancing at the NCO club. I learned to slip past security as Ken's guest, a small act of camaraderie that brightened long, rigorous days.

One Saturday, after an indulgent evening with Ken in Asbury Park, I signed the wake-up log for KP duty. I adjusted the wake-up times discreetly. I was assigned as the dining room orderly—a role with breakfast duty from 5:00 to 11:00 a.m. About 9:00 a.m., I lined up chairs behind a table, and succumbing to a brief nap. The mess sergeant bellowed, "Where's the dining room orderly?" I scrambled to offer a half-truth—that was my final attempt at the chair-napping routine.

By September, as the Berlin Crisis escalated, I was deployed to Fort Bliss near El Paso for the Missile Master program. After a three-month Fire Unit Integration Facility course, I became an instructor for two years—a Signal Corps assignment under the Air Defense Command that allowed me a light ten-hour workweek and precious time to resume my college engineering studies.

At Fort Bliss, life balanced discipline with small escapes. Monthly trips to Ciudad Juárez for 25-cent tequila shots, hearty steaks, and spicy chili punctuated my days, while Friday and Saturday dances at the NCO Club, renowned for its hamburgers, lifted our spirits on scorching summers. I often retreated to a cool lounge—the Green Frog across from the downtown park—with friends like Paul Repko and Ken Carpenter, one of whom once saved me from alcohol poisoning. I still wonder how I let that happen.

One afternoon, while overseeing a lab with fellow instructors, Paul convinced me to grab a quick beer and join him for a pool game at the PX. By 5:00 p.m., I reemerged reeking of beer and dizzy in the hot sun. The course sergeant glimpsed my appearance and wondered how I was drinking beer in the lab.

I met Betty, the sister of an army friend visiting from Springfield, Illinois. After exchanging letters and spending a week on leave with her, I learned she was entangled in another relationship. As I headed back to Fort Bliss, I said, "You will never marry that guy!" Years later, I'd flip through the Springfield phone book and find her name still there unmarried, a quiet testament to fate's own pacing.

From September until my discharge, I was named "Instructor of the Month" three times—a hard-won honor amid the rigors of training. My service ended on December 2, 1963. Dreams of Fort Bliss haunted me over the next few years as I tried to explain, "I had served my time."

Note: During my Army years, I meticulously planned for my return to college. My real breakthrough in engineering came in 1972 when I prepared for the professional engineering exam in Ohio. For nearly a year, I attacked complex problems three nights a week. Of the 2,000 engineers taking the test, the top score was 84; I earned a 78—well above the 70 needed to pass. I might have done even better had I remembered my compass for those tricky resonance circuit problems that demanded a graphical solution.

MENDING A LIFE

By December, after my discharge, I was back at the Free Press, attending classes at Lawrence Tech, living with my parents, and driving my dad's 1955 Pontiac. Sam had also returned from California and found work at a Shell garage near Allen Park, making support payments for earlier missteps.

About a year before leaving the service, I took leave and met with Mr. Hancock, dean of the Electrical Engineering Department, to discuss returning to Lawrence Tech. Typically, an extended gap in classes called for remedial work, but I persuaded Mr. Hancock to let me pick up where I left off.

My course load was manageable, with only two quarters left to finish the 24 credits I needed. On Wednesday evenings, I visited a psychologist to address my depression. Although I qualified for GI Bill assistance, I had come this far on my own and intended to finish that way. I saw Sam about once a week, but my main priority was earning my degree.

In May, I got a job offer from Boeing in New Orleans, and by June, I had earned my Bachelor of Science in Electrical Engineering. After cashing in my Army savings bonds, I paid my father for room and board from December through June. He was reluctant to take the money, and I saw tears in his eyes.

I bought a used Buick from my Uncle John and prepared for my next journey. One afternoon, I visited Sam, using the $25 he'd paid me for the Pontiac on drinks. A few nights later, I called Betty in Springfield to ask if she'd join me in New Orleans, but she declined.

At last, I was on my way. Glancing in the rearview mirror, I caught a fleeting glimpse of my past—memories, people, and experiences that had shaped my life.

AN ASSESSMENT AT TWENTY-SEVEN

Looking back now, I realize my early struggles weren't just bad luck—they were the product of growing up without a mentor. My father had barely finished third grade, and my mother stopped after eighth, leaving me to navigate school on my own while my siblings were preoccupied with their own lives. I stumbled through lessons, never learning the art of study or retention.

Hands-on classes like art, music, gym, and shop came easily—each a burst of color and movement. But math, reading, and grammar demanded a focus I didn't yet know how to master. I struggled to teach myself how to read and I recall the rough but earnest way my father taught me to count change when collecting milk bills.

High school, however, brought a few guiding voices. Mrs. Elton drilled tenth-grade grammar into us with relentless patience, and our neighbor, Mrs. Larson, sat with me after school to untangle algebraic puzzles. Mr. Parish's twelfth-grade physics lessons—part demonstration, part conversation—hinted at a world governed by laws I could grasp. Their words helped, though by graduation I still had only the bare minimum for college and my dreams in music felt uncertain. Then came the aptitude test, a moment when everything pivoted. In mere seconds, the test reimagined my future, pointing me toward engineering—a path I had never considered but one that lit a spark inside me.

I applied to Lawrence Tech, passed the entrance exam, and that fall I stepped into classrooms where equations promised a new language of understanding. Even as I juggled an 18-credit schedule, worked nights, and stretched every dollar to cover tuition and room and board, I began to see the faint outline of a future I could shape. I received no handouts from my siblings, and the shadow of the draft board loomed, threatening to derail my efforts.

By my third year, late-night study sessions shifted into deep conversations with books of existential philosophy. I'd pore over *Existentialism and Religious Beliefs*, the words of Sartre, Camus, and even Schopenhauer echoing in the quiet hours. Their ideas gave shape to my doubts and bolstered my resolve, preparing me, unknowingly, for challenges yet to come.

In December 1960, I lost my deferment and was drafted into the Army—an event that, strangely, saved me. Military life pulled me into electronics school and later to instructing in the Signal Corps at Fort Bliss, Texas. The strict routines and unexpected camaraderie honed parts of me I never knew existed. When I was discharged in December 1963, I returned to the familiar hum of the Detroit Free Press Advertising Department. By January, I was back in class, and in June 1964, I finally earned my BSEE.

Around that time, old habits crept back in. Sam reappeared, and I found myself drinking again—sometimes too much—while seeking refuge in weekly sessions with a psychologist. Yet even amidst the turbulence, I kept my coursework steady long enough to accept a job that whisked me away to New Orleans, far from my old life.

Now, standing at twenty-seven, I see a tapestry woven from all those fractured threads—lonely classrooms, late-night equations, the steady guidance of a few dedicated teachers, the harsh discipline of the Army, and the bittersweet taste of early independence. I have no regrets. Every mishap, every struggle taught me something, even if it felt like stumbling in the dark at the time. Each experience, painful or small, nudged me along a path that, despite its twists, led me to where I am today—and hinted at the promise of a future I was only beginning to imagine.

Summer 1938: Gerry, Wally, Rosemary & Bobby (Front)

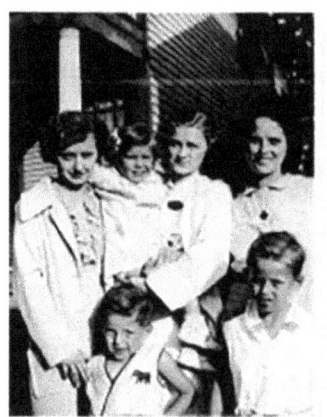

Spring 1936: Cassie, Wanda & Sylvia–
Wally, Rosemary & Gerry

Summer 1941: Snapshot Bobby– Bobby & Walter

Friends: Mickey, Bobby & Jack– Bobby 41, 44& 48

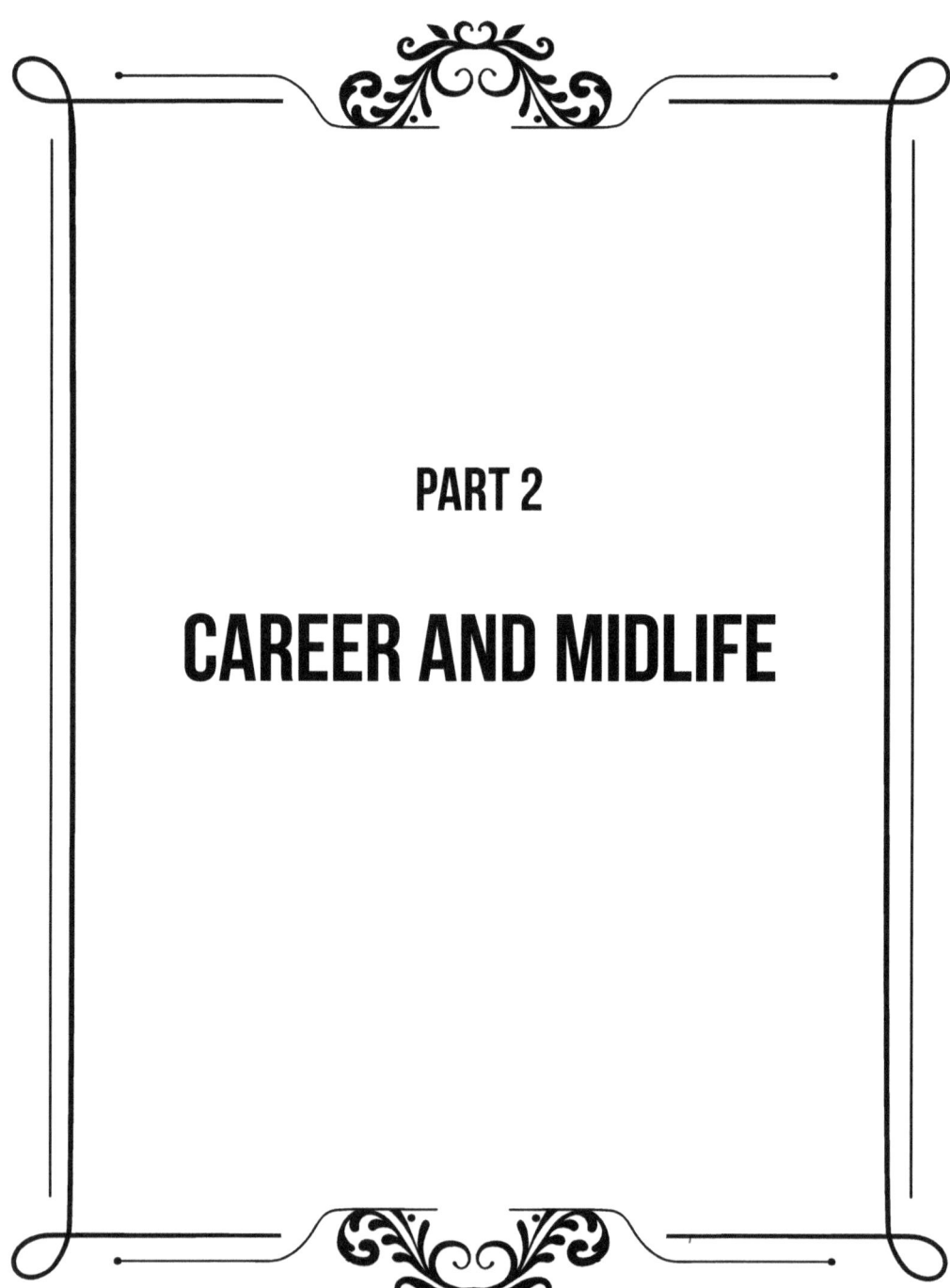

PART 2

CAREER AND MIDLIFE

NEW ORLEANS- 1964

The journey south from Detroit took two days along worn highways and through sleepy rural towns. With only partially finished interstates and palpable tension in the Deep South—where the Ku Klux Klan and wary police cast long shadows—I felt eyes tracking my Michigan plates. Relief finally hit as I crossed the causeway from Covington into New Orleans, and I was greeted by warm, open faces unlike those I had left behind.

My first night in a modest motel gave way to a new, vibrant world. I quickly secured a room in a grand old house on City Park Avenue, right across from the storied dueling oaks of City Park. Sundays melted into long hours wandering beneath the moss-draped oaks, catching spontaneous film screenings at the Delgado Art Museum, sipping rich coffee in the French Quarter, and riding the streetcar along St. Charles Avenue past elegant mansions and buzzing university streets. Even a simple meal—a homemade French dinner for seventy-five cents at a corner shop—became a cherished taste of this near-perfect city.

At Boeing's Michoud facility in New Orleans East, where we built the S-IC stage for the Saturn V rocket, I worked as a planner on the Time Clock Generator for the Cape launch system. The manufacturing floor pulsed with activity—a mix of precise engineering and everyday banter. Among the secretaries (jokingly dubbed "sexataries" by the crew) scanning for northern charm, I met Linda. Her confident glance and ready smile sparked something unexpected.

A few months later, I transferred to Huntsville, and before long, Linda and I were married. I still recall her firm retort when I suggested waiting to settle down:

"Not a chance, Bob."

Our ceremony, hastily performed by Willy Smith—a justice of the peace in Poplarville, Mississippi—echoed an old warning: "Sin in haste, and repent at leisure."

HUNTSVILLE— GETTING STARTED

In early December, I moved to Huntsville. I rented a small room near Five Points on Pratt Avenue, a temporary perch before finding an apartment at 708 Maysville Road. I scavenged through the local paper for used furniture—a full living room, kitchen, and bedroom set for a mere $125. I held onto cherished pieces long after our return to New Orleans in 1974. I even clung to a pricey portable Singer sewing machine, its price tag now a bittersweet reminder of promises never fulfilled.

Home life, however, brought its own turbulence. One evening, as I sat at the kitchen table with a sink brimming with dishes, I gently told Linda they needed washing. In one flash, her eyes darkened. A fist swung in anger; I caught it in my peripheral vision, twisting her arm in a reflex to defuse the blow. "You hurt me!" she cried, voice trembling as I retorted, "I'd be on the floor if you'd landed that punch." That was only Round One in a series of clashes that would punctuate our life together.

At Boeing, I worked in the Hicks Building's engineering department, focusing on measurement analysis for rocket engines—a job that felt increasingly trivial as I watched my colleagues loiter and joke in the corridors. Then Bob DeRose, a physicist on the cusp of a new career with General Electric in Cincinnati, made me realize it was time to move on. Offers trickled in from New England and Nevada, but one flight in particular rattled my nerves—a Martin 440 out of Atlanta sputtered an engine right after takeoff, forcing us back to the terminal amid panicked passengers. Still, GE in Cincinnati ultimately called. After an initial interview with Bernie Burdick and a follow-up call that explained a promising new role in instrumentation and facility engineering, I accepted and prepared to start in two weeks. That decision led to eight years of fascinating projects, a stable income, and the slow, painful unfolding of family life.

GREENHILLS

Linda, our one-year-old daughter Andrea, and I eventually settled in northern Cincinnati. We began in a rented apartment in Forest Park before buying a modest house in Greenhills near Winton Woods State Park. At GE's Large Jet Engine Development Group, I was busy at work, but I soon realized I hadn't yet seen the full scars Linda carried. In New Orleans, she'd described a childhood filled with isolation and harsh treatment—a quiet litany of bullying, broken promises, and even a suicide attempt that left its mark. Why wasn't I paying attention?

Outwardly, Linda remained bright, witty, and in control, but our partnership often felt unbalanced. There was difficulty as she struggled with the responsibilities of motherhood, demanding I take time off from work to help her with the kids or drive her across town to a doctor's appointment. There would be moments when her anger erupted—my narrowly averting her long nails, restraining her as she raged. When Daniel arrived, we were clinging to the appearance of a happy family while our private battles continued on. At company functions, we smiled for the cameras, while our bridge group voted us "the couple most likely to divorce."

Linda pursued her own ambitions: writing weekly columns for the *Greenhills Journal* and running for city council. I urged her to run in a local district where her face was familiar, but a last-minute attack letter cost her an at-large race by a mere fifteen votes. A year after moving into our Greenhills home, the weight of our mistakes pressed down on me. With two children and mounting doubts, I asked myself, "How do I fix this?"

Time passed slowly. By spring 1974, I began attending transactional analysis sessions, grappling with the fractured pieces of my life. The decision to leave GE, sell our home, and uproot our lives emerged gradually until, by October, a new job offer finally charted the course. It was enough to send me, Linda, and the kids back to New Orleans, where I hoped a fresh start might mend old wounds.

In every mile traveled, every car repair and doctor's office visits, every sleepless night and tentative new beginning, New Orleans remained the ever-present promise of renewal. Even when dark moments in personal life threatened to overwhelm me, the music of the city—the echoing brass on Bourbon Street, the quiet wisdom of historic neighborhoods— whispered of redemption and the possibility of change.

GENERAL ELECTRIC'S LARGE JET ENGINE DEVELOPMENT GROUP

After leaving Huntsville and Boeing, I spent eight years at GE—a period during which my Army-honed skills in electronics and digital logic became invaluable. In Facilities Engineering, I designed systems that captured jet engine test data for military and commercial programs. I worked first under Bernie Burdick, then under Burt Fister, one of GE's finest engineers. Fister rarely approached me directly; instead, he'd send another engineer to test my ideas, and within days I'd be drafting solutions and securing budgets. My projects spanned major programs—TF39, CF6, GE4, LM2500, F100—and included a Precision Torque Measurement System that eliminated water-brake cavitation and achieved 0.001% precision, and an Advanced Diagnostic Engine Monitoring System for the C-5A that foreshadowed today's commercial systems.

Until I turned thirty-seven, my career trajectory was steep. Then one day, George Moore, my boss, mentioned that Fister had called me "lucky," adding, "He wouldn't say shit if he had a mouth full of it." At that point, GE's cost-cutting drive was forcing seasoned engineers aside—Vince Trainor was forced out, and Floyd Nesbett's pay was slashed. I had been quietly job-hunting when a New Orleans opportunity appeared. Years earlier, I'd warned Bernie never to pair me with Wayne—someone who'd once taken credit for my work. So when George revealed that Fister planned to assign me and Wayne to a new remote test project, I snapped, "George, you have my resignation effective in two weeks." When George passed the word to Fister, his only response was a curt, "Shit!"

Before leaving GE, I forged a friendship with Bob Falcone, an electronic technician whose humor and outrageous stories—like a chance encounter with Arnold Schwarzenegger at a nudist camp—still brighten my phone calls. Even after my departure, I occasionally visited Fister in Ohio. Before George died, he confided that I was on track to be the next unit manager, but by then, my path had already taken another turn.

BACK TO NEW ORLEANS- 1974

At thirty-seven, I returned to New Orleans, stepping into the petroleum industry with a blend of relief and trepidation. My brother-in-law, Bill Watts, passed along my résumé to CAC, and soon I was interviewing with Bill D., a mechanical engineer from A&M. Teaming up with an experienced colleague, I dove into a project supplying instrumentation and electrical equipment for nineteen 3,000 horsepower gas turbine compressor modules destined for Brunei and the world's largest LNG facility. The project was challenging—structural work was performed on the Houston Ship Channel at Cardinal Industries.

Every other week, I was in Houston—overseeing the project and negotiating change orders with Solar Turbines and Cardinal Industries. In New Orleans, I was handling purchasing and supervising shop assembly and testing of control equipment for the modules. I shared an apartment in Houston with Gary Beaty, a capable supervisor of a small crew whose casual habit of stirring trouble soon confronted me. One summer morning, when Linda and I arrived at our shared apartment, a disheveled blonde answered door in nothing but underwear. Linda's voice cut through the scene: "You are not staying here!" On another occasion, Gary tried to push an attractive newcomer onto me—an idea I quickly rejected.

The tension wasn't confined to work. At home, our marriage frayed under the weight of constant travel and mounting stress. After we bought a house on the West Bank in Aurora, Linda began turning the kids against me. One night in our upstairs bedroom, overwhelmed, I broke down and offered her the house, the car, everything—just to end the misery. She coldly replied that I'd have to take the kids, a decision that seemed impossible given my demanding schedule.

By October, the Houston project was nearing completion. I remembered lunch and a surreal night: after a crew party that dragged on until 4:00 a.m., I drove a Louisiana farm girl home and was pulled over in La Porte. Half-drunk yet composed, I was let go—a small, unforgettable moment. As I flew back to New Orleans at dawn, I kept thinking who at CAC wouuld approve that $1,000 "lunch" expense and about that chance enounter with that Louisiana farm girl (educational).

Three months later, I was on a Pan Am flight from San Francisco to Brunei, with stops in Hawaii, Guam, and Singapore. In Brunei, I was tasked with fine-tuning the speed control and adjustments to anti-surge systems on the compressor modules. Staying in Kuala Belait beside a Chinese cemetery, I endured daily funerals with ceaseless nightly prayers and chanting, a relentless echo of loss that robbed me of sleep. One morning, while adjusting to left-side driving, I passed riverbank workers swinging eight-foot poles with knives; by evening, I saw a fourteen-foot cobra dangle from a tree limb. Later, an NOC engineer named Lex Van Hoven invited me for dinner at his house—built on pilings with a small monkey named Mickey chained as a watchdog. Mickey'd go berserk at the mere hint of a snake, a story Lex recounted with a wry smile.

My Brunei chapter wasn't without peril. Missing the chopper to the APC-6, I took a boat to a maintenance ship and then a rickety plank to the platform's understructure—crawling on hands and knees as Chinese laborers chuckled overhead. Later, when my 30-day tourist visa ran short, I drove a coastal jungle road with a young mechanic, marveling at Asian children in huts and fish displayed in open markets until I spent the Chinese New Year in Bandar Seri Begawan before returning via Hong Kong.

I still recall arriving back home: Frisky, our little dog—a gift from Linda's mother—leaped joyfully at the door, while Linda and the kids offered nothing but distant silence. "Hi Frisky!" I'd call, finding solace in the uncomplicated joy of a loyal pet.

CAC— SETTLING IN

After the Brunei project, Terry appointed me lead electrical engineer at CAC. I managed projects with little real authority, often shouldering blame for delays. On Christmas Eve, when I asked friend Bob Smith to plan an offshore start-up, Bob snapped, "Get fucked!" A week later, as Terry discussed another project, I stunned him by announcing, "I'm stepping down as the electrical manager—I want to run my own jobs." Terry's surprise, and the subsequent half-bonus cut, after Bill D., the VP of Engineering, was consulted—brought me a small victory in regaining control. From that moment, tasks were mine to choose.

Personnel shifts soon brought relief. Doug M., the VP of Marketing, exited around 1980, and Charlie F. stepped in. At one point, they even considered me for head of engineering after Bill and Terry left to start Petro-xyz with Doug, but I declined—I wasn't ready for that kind of headache. I'd planned a two-week vacation with Linda before a start-up on Eugene Island 342 that Terry was scheduled to perform. Terry forced me to work three rainy weeks offshore doing the start-up. Later, he tried to make it up to me with paid time off. I always admired Terry's straightforwardness; later at Petro-xyz he tried repeatedly to hire me, but I'd grown too attached to my newfound independence with Charlie.

In the early '80s, life on the side was a mix of golf, excessive drinking, and rough camaraderie with Joe and George, two retired Coast Guardsmen. We played tournaments, sometimes leaving the Bayou Barriere Golf Club in a haze of drunken laughter. One night, Joe urinated on the back of my car—an absurd, comic moment that still makes me shake my head. At another golf outing, after a morning of continuous drinking, a police officer tailed us for miles, waiting for me to make a misstep. Then, on a slow, rainy evening at a tiny pizza joint on Barataria Boulevard, I was pulled over—only to have the officer help me locate my driver's license in my wallet and let me off with a warning.

For most of my life, I'd been a social drinker—never too far past moderation. But one night, while driving the Greater New Orleans Bridge, I realized I was flirting with disaster—a near miss with a DWI. That night, I resolved: no more than two beers or a glass of wine, ever again. Later, with DeLinda I quit altogether; with Linh in California, a glass or two accompanied Texas Hold'em; now in Foley, I occasionally share a beer with my brothers-in-law—but nothing more.

Throughout it all—from the buzzing corridors of GE and the high-stakes projects in Houston and Brunei to the fragile balances of marriage and the reckless nights on New Orleans streets—I learned that success and survival often hinge on both technical skill and personal resilience. Every decision, every misadventure, and every moment of unexpected connection steered me toward a future I never could have mapped out in my youth. In the relentless clatter of engines, in the roar of oil money, and in the soft, persistent jazz that drifts over Bourbon Street, I found reminders that even amidst chaos, there's always a chance for renewal.

MEXICO, 1980–1982

After Bill and Terry left to start Petro-xyz with Doug, Charlie shifted our company's focus from compressor controls to manufacturing multiwell control panels, Bourdon tube pressure pilots, and control valves. He brought in Pedro as our South American marketing rep and Gianluca as our agent in Mexico City. Late in 1980, I was assigned a technical support role in Mexico City. CAC was then supplying multiwell hydraulic control panels for almost thirty Gulf of Mexico platforms, and I added a Platform Alarm and Shutdown Panel with a telemetry interface to each.

I began flying to Mexico City every other Monday on Eastern Airlines from New Orleans. Staying at the luxurious El Presidente Chapultepec Hotel in Polanco, I found myself swept up by a world where work and pleasure blurred seamlessly. Mornings meant technical meetings with Pedro and Pemex engineers; afternoons, impromptu siestas in sunlit corridors; and nights, vibrant excursions through clubs and restaurants. One evening, over a few drinks, Pedro nudged me to approach a captivating woman at a club. "Just say, 'Te quiero mucho,'" he urged. That simple phrase broke the ice, and soon, Sonia Zamora and I were inseparable for months. We traversed Mexico together—driving through Cuernavaca and Cocoyoc, even staying at a 1920s country home once owned by President Díaz. I vividly remember arriving one Saturday, only to be greeted at the airport by Sonia and a full mariachi band.

Yet amid the leisure, danger lurked. I toured hazardous oil and gas sites—from offshore platforms in the Bay of Campeche to facilities in Ciudad del Carmen, Reynosa, and Nuevo Laredo—where high H_2S levels and scant safety gear were a daily risk. I recall an office visit with Pemex's president: as he recounted an inspection on a platform where a safety vent valve to the flare stack had been blocked. Noting the danger, he left immediately. I appreciated his candor.

On another trip, a misadventure at Ciudad del Carmen turned surreal. A captain at immigration seized my passport, and I later found myself "hot-sheeting" it in a seedy brothel once the night had run its course. Another evening, missing breakfast on a rushed flight, I spent the day sipping Galliano with a non–English-speaking engineer until Pedro, Gianluca, and I wrapped up the night at Susan's—a high-end brothel for the well-to-do—before I spent a miserable morning reeling from dry heaves at the El Presidente. Even in these chaotic moments, there were fleeting pockets of humor: once, Charlie was in town for a visit and while we sipped cocktails in the lobby to soft piano melodies, he joked that Gianluca's breath was powerful enough to peel wallpaper.

Pedro and I, ever the adventurers, would dine in Zona Rosa or at La Fonda del Recuerdo. There, we savored a bowl of exquisite sopa mariscos and sipped a curious cocktail called El Torito, its tiny seed a mild, almost hypnotic distraction. Business ambitions also ran high—Pedro, Gianluca, and I started a Louisiana company to market instrumentation in Mexico, though my partners often prioritized other ventures. I once secured a solid lead for selling tank gauging equipment outside Mexico City, only to lose the deal as our contact went direct. Later, at an OTC conference in Houston, the company's rep thanked me with a firm handshake—a quiet tribute to missed opportunities.

Pedro and Gianluca's long-shared history surfaced in brief stories: Pedro recalled how Gianluca once boated prostitutes to offshore platforms to win contracts, and in his early days, Pedro himself had smuggled currency hidden in car tires into Ecuador. Business with Pemex surged—until the 1982 election. A few days before the vote, Pemex's purchasing records on the fourth and seventh floors of the Pemex office building were firebombed overnight, erasing years of wellhead and telemetry data. Soon after, Mexico's economic collapse sent the peso plummeting from 23 to 2,000 per U.S. dollar. Pedro once made the fatal error of hailing a street cab instead of using hotel transport; he was robbed, abandoned at the city dump in his underwear. Expensive clothes and flashy jewelry were no longer safe. I began dressing casually, hiding my watch in my pocket, and eventually convinced Charlie to have Miguel, a Chilean, take over my trips. My focus then shifted to trips to Brazil, Trinidad, and Venezuela.

(Note: Early oil production in the Bay of Campeche had outstripped the platform test separators' design capacity. I designed a multiphase flow measurement system using a sampling technique that CAC patented—but never developed further. Seven years later, a major Houston oilfield service company adopted and deployed the concept.)

Back in New Orleans, I resumed engineering work with United Gas Pipeline, developed innovative products for domestic oil production—solar-powered, all-hydraulic well control panels for Aramco, Abu Dhabi, and Dubai. Today, companies in the Middle East manufacture similar panels locally.

I also put my personal life into order. I enrolled Linda at Holy Cross College in New Orleans, where she tackled an 18-hour course load to earn her degree in education—and later, a master's in gifted education from UNO—while teaching full-time. With her busy schedule, she had little time to monitor my travels. One day, she found my American Express statement and, comparing my Mexican expenses with our family budget at home, remarked on the extravagant differences. I could only reply, "You should've become an engineer instead of a teacher." Eventually, I took her on one of my trips to Mexico City, and she finally grasped the allure of five-star living.

A SECOND ROUND

After Brunei, I worked on several projects over the next few years—supplying instrumentation and electrical controls for turbine compressors for Amoco Trinidad and Gulf Grand Bay, gas metering panels, pump control panels for Aramco, and a 48-point benzene gas detection system for the Union Carbide Plant in Taft, Louisiana.

In 1979, I began work on the Vinton Compressor Station for UGPL, located about four miles east of the Texas–Louisiana border near I-10. This land-based facility housed three Centaur turbine compressors in parallel, featuring capacity control and auto start/stop, with Gary Beaty once again leading the crew. The project went well, and I established a strong working relationship with Farrell Adams and Nick Schaefer—a former World War II artillery captain. This connection led to a series of projects over the next seven years, including a new 750-million-standard-cubic-feet-per-day (SCFD) glycol dehydration plant for the Lake Bistineau Compressor Station and upgrades to the existing dry bed treatment units.

Lake Bistineau was a major underground gas storage facility near Shreveport, used to store offshore gas during the spring, summer, and fall. In winter, it drew gas from the field to supplement the offshore supply—sometimes reaching a flow of nearly two billion SCFD in a 30-inch pipeline at 900 psi to the Midwest. Dehydration of the gas was crucial to prevent freezing of downstream controls and instruments along the distribution network. A few years ago (circa 2020), Texas power companies neglected this detail, leading to winter power outages and staggering electricity bills.

Later, I worked on the J.C. Nelson Compressor Station, the Katy Compressor Station, and several Pemex and Aramco projects, developing innovative technology products for well control with remote telemetry.

I remember my father's words when I was struggling in college: "All work and no play makes Jack a dull boy." I survived those years, and eventually I began improving my social skills—attending parties, golfing on Wednesday afternoons and Saturday mornings with A.J., and playing rounds at Beau Chene across the lake with Clark and Julian. Sometimes I'd have lunch at the Sea Train Bar down the street, shooting pool and throwing darts. The Sea Train had a rough atmosphere— broken bar stools, cold beer in the summer, and Merrill and Larry making shrimp po'boys. Larry once upgraded the place by buying new barstools, which changed the ambiance so much that we stopped going for several weeks while he tried to figure out what had happened.

On Friday nights, the regulars from engineering were joined by the marketing team, and we'd stay until ten or eleven. I advised Linda never to call me at the Train on Friday nights. One evening, she did call and ended up speaking with Gary. I refused to answer, and after that, Gary made it a point to steer clear of her.

Friday afternoons, I would relax and light a mild, flared-tip Cuban cigar in my office. Later, after Bill and Terry left the company and started Petro-xyz with Doug, I began spending Friday nights with the marketing group—Charlie, Ronnie Guarino, Bob Howell, and Pedro—at Chi-Chi's. On weekday evenings, I was usually at home, working on the house, playing bridge with Linda's friends, or spending time with the kids.

There was an older gentleman, Warren Breau, in charge of personnel, who had a knack for hiring only young, attractive, unattached women for the office staff. As Preston would say, "Only thoroughbreds."

On occasion, Vernon, the marketing manager, would throw parties at his apartment on the west bank, inviting most of the marketing staff. I was particularly fond of one girl, Amy. One night, while wearing a T-shirt, she fell into the pool. Wet, she walked over to where I was sitting on the sofa, perched briefly on the armrest before rolling over on top of me. With Linda standing just a few feet away, I quickly said,

"Amy, I'd like you to meet my wife, Linda." Linda smirked and replied, "Fried eggs!"

A few weeks later, I was at Scratches Bar with Pedro, Jim, and Ronnie, dancing with Amy, when Linda unexpectedly walked in—with her hair in curlers. She made a beeline for me and Amy. Pedro, Jim, and Ronnie vanished—either ducking under the table or hiding behind a pitcher of beer. Linda tapped me on the back. I hadn't seen her enter. Startled, I turned and said, "You remember Amy?" She simply said, "Let's go."

On the drive home, Linda called me a few names and made some accusations. I replied, "What are you going to do about it?" That moment became a turning point in our relationship. Now in college, Linda realized that control in our marriage wasn't solely in her hands. She later admitted that she had planned to throw me out but first wanted to make me stay. She lost weight, took better care of herself, and started treating me differently. Over the next twenty-five years, we found our way back to each other, learning to share and love again—though distractions continued. I could never really live with someone seven days a week, week after week.

During Linda's college years, there were other challenging moments, but things were gradually improving. Bob Smith, who worked with me in engineering, and I would occasionally stop for beers after work. One evening, I came home drunk with him. Linda had planned a dinner for the next night with friends from Holy Cross College and had reminded me several times of its importance. The next day, Bob drove me home without any stops, and I had to finish some electrical wiring diagrams for the shop.

"Bob, when we get to my house, let's pretend we're drunk and see how Linda reacts," I suggested. We staggered through the door. I placed my documents on the kitchen counter, where Linda was preparing dinner. She took one look, swept everything off the counter, and sent my paperwork flying against the wall in a crumpled pile. Bob stood there, shocked.

"Linda, Bob and I were just kidding," I said. Regaining her composure, she replied, "So was I."

Another time, after Linda had graduated from college and was about to start her master's degree at UNO, she took a teaching job at Belle Chasse Middle School, teaching fourth grade. She came home with her first paycheck, waving it in the air. "Haha, this is mine," she said with a hint of independence. I retorted, "No, you owe me Twenty-Five Thousand Dollars." She then threw the check at me.

"Look," I said, "take the credit cards and spend what you want, but deposit the checks into the bank for Andrea's and Daniel's college fund—they'll be starting soon!" We were establishing new respect and boundaries in our relationship.

Office gossip and eccentricities abounded too. A.J. hired a new secretary, a striking woman whose wild personal life became fodder for our marketing team's dry humor. One day, after she transferred to marketing, her replacement doused everything in Lysol—a bizarre attempt to sanitize our chaotic reality. Drugs sometimes surfaced; I recall softly greeting a secretary known as "the Snow Queen," only for her to hush me with a resigned, "Bob, cut it out." Despite it all, moments of genuine connection peppered the routine—like sharing a quiet drink at the bar with Charlie's secretary, whose soft laughter and knowing glances still echo in my memory.

Looking back now, through the haze of long nights and near-misses with both fate and a DWI, I realize that my journey through Mexico, the CAC years, and beyond was a relentless dance between risk and reward. In every meeting, in every precarious project, even in the quiet moments spent nursing a beer or a Cuban cigar, the universe was urging me onward. The echoes of mariachi bands in Mexico City, the muted laughter at Susan's, and the stark reality of business deals gone awry were all signposts directing me toward a future I was only beginning to grasp—a future that, no matter the setbacks and scars, promised renewal in every challenging step.

And through it all, I continued learning—both as an engineer and as a man—always aware that every triumph and every misadventure was an integral note in the symphony of my life.

GLOBAL TRAVELS

My travel experiences began with trips through the Detroit–Windsor tunnel and occasional jaunts to Ciudad Juárez. Then, in January 1976 at age thirty-eight, I embarked on my first major international journey—Brunei. The thrill wasn't just in the destination; it was in every unexpected stop along the way: the vibrant energy of Hawaii, the bustling streets of Singapore and Hong Kong, and the foggy charm of San Francisco. Jet lag stole days from my schedule, but every lost hour was repaid in wonder.

In subsequent years, my itineraries spanned Mexico, Brazil, Venezuela, Trinidad, both coasts of Canada, Nova Scotia, England, Scotland, much of Europe, Indonesia, the Middle East, Latin America, and even Alaska—all driven by equal parts business necessity and personal curiosity. New Orleans became my home base for these adventures, with Houston serving as the launching pad for frequent trips. Forty years of shuttling between these cities—even nine years of weekly flights—left me with sleepless nights and a permanent buzz of anticipation.

BRAZIL

After many trips in Mexico, I found myself in Rio de Janeiro, where I was sent to meet Alex—a retired Chilean Navy captain and our company's corporate representative. My assignment was to prepare a proposal for a fire suppression system on the Petrobras Enchova Platform. One day, while touring an engineering firm, a New York expatriate greeted us with a curt, "What's in it for me?" Later at Petrobras, a local engineer insulted Alex. I told Alex later, "If we want this job, we'll need to win over his associate."

The next day in São Paulo, we assessed a support facility's ability to install our system, and a few weeks later I returned with the proposal. Back in New Orleans, a vice president from a major fire suppression company demanded a 5% commission—which was promptly refused.

In a cruel twist of fate, about ten years later, a fire on that very platform claimed the lives of twelve workers.

The city itself cast a spell: Rio's striking landmarks—its opera house, cathedral, and other architectural marvels—stirred something deep within me. I remember the music on the street, the soft crash of waves at Atlantica Beach, and the aroma of freshly brewed coffee. Yet even on my first day, caution was the word: just a day after my arrival, tourists in the hotel next to mine were robbed at gunpoint. The hotel staff's warnings to avoid bringing valuables to the beach would stay with me for years.

VENEZUELA

A trip to Venezuela remains vivid in my memory. I was sent to meet Petroleos de Venezuela's technical team in Morichal, with stops in Maracaibo and Caracas along the way. In Morichal, I stayed in a modest hotel for only ten dollars a night—its bar opened all night, though my room quickly proved infested with cockroaches. The next morning, on route to an engineering office, I passed a mud pit volcano—a bubbling chasm that swallowed an entire drilling rig, trucks, and crew in minutes. By late afternoon, I found myself in Caracas where better accommodations offered a brief reprieve from the harshness of the field.

ANCHORAGE AND PRUDHOE BAY, ALASKA

Vernon, CAC's marketing manager asked me to fly to Prudhoe Bay to meet a British oil company's production engineer about a forty-well chemical injection system. It was February, and as I arrived in Anchorage, the chill was bone-dry, accentuated by a ten-foot stuffed grizzly bear looming in the Hilton's lobby. Anchorage was a city of contrasts—world-class seafood restaurants nestled amongst icy streets. The next day, after reviewing the site at Prudhoe Bay, I devised a cost-saving plan. The engineer promised CAC would get the order, but our proposal was later handed off to our main competitor by a shrewd purchasing agent—a lesson in the treachery of oil business that recalled the Deepwater Horizon debacle years later.

THE MIDDLE EAST

By the mid-1980s, I was pursuing an idea to replace natural gas with solar power and hydraulic fluid as a control medium. Fred Johnson sent me to Saudi Arabia, where I discussed a prototype dual-well package for Aramco's Saffaniyah 111/138 platform. I spent nearly a year shuttling to Dhahran on extended trips. The system featured UHF radio link that bridged a ten-mile gap between the production office and the platform. The project culminated in success after long days in the region. I later handled projects in Dubai, Abu Dhabi, and Bahrain—places of stark contrasts, where European-style restaurants offered beer and wine despite strict local prohibitions. On my final trip to Saudi Arabia, an ill-judged purchase of alcoholic chocolate in London got me detained and fined—a bitter reminder that some lines, once crossed, aren't easily redrawn. I recall another night playing poker with fellow Americans at camp, only to quit early after detecting subtle cheating—a microcosm of the risks in a region that both captivated and cautioned me.

TRINIDAD AND TOBAGO

In the late 1980s, I engineered an offshore production management project for Trinmar at Point Fortin. Transforming an old drilling rig into an oil production platform. The system managed remote control of two heavy oil pumps and a satellite platform from an onshore computer. In San Fernando, near Point Fortin, I experienced the vibrant local culture—a quirky "upside-down" Hilton with buzzing Saturday parties, tin bands, and endless tropical weekends. Yet danger followed me even here. Before completing the project, I slipped while boarding a boat in rough seas and sustained a bilateral inguinal hernia, which later forced me into surgery. A bout with parasites from contaminated food required a course of medication. Although Trinidad's beauty was undeniable, its wild side—accentuated by alarming AIDS rates and risky sexual habits—cast a long shadow.

EUROPE

Travel in Europe often blended business with personal indulgences. CAC's Richmond office saw me drafting commercial proposals for Norwegian equipment while I spent long lunch breaks betting on horses around the corner. I recall a two-week stint working on a proposal with Richard Tullis, punctuated by an endless flow of ale and cider. In North Yorkshire, I stayed at the Black Swan Inn near Kirkbymoorside, sharing a luncheon with a distinguished marine engineer whose quiet command of history and craft left a lasting impression. Personal trips with Linda, DeLinda, and Linh brought me to York, the moors of Wuthering Heights, Scotland, Germany, Switzerland, Belgium, Italy, France, and Spain. London, Amsterdam, Munich, and Berlin became my favorite cities—especially the tiny beer garden across from the ring fountain in Nuremberg with its little German sausages, sauerkraut, and beer, a simple pleasure I highly recommend.

REFLECTIONS ON GLOBAL JOURNEYS

Every journey etched its own lesson in my memory: the hidden perils of oil production sites, the camaraderie formed over late-night drinks in bustling clubs, and the quiet wonder of new cultures. I learned early on that travel was as much about navigating danger as it was about embracing beauty—the seized passport in Ciudad del Carmen, a near-miss with flying on a Martin 440, or the biting cold of Alaska's Prudhoe Bay all intertwined with moments of unexpected warmth. I gathered experiences from every corner of the globe, each a thread in the tapestry of my life—a tapestry that, even amid turmoil and broken promises, began to reveal the contours of a future laden with possibility. And as I continued to trace my steps—from New Orleans and Houston to Rio and Riyadh—I realized that every misadventure, every delighted conversation over a cocktail or shared joke in a streetcar, was quietly preparing me for the next step along this winding, remarkable journey.

ZERO VISIBILITY - AN END TO FUN AND GAMES

In 1986, I returned to New Orleans fresh off a long stint in Saudi Arabia, where I'd wrapped up work on a Solar Power All-Hydraulic Dual Well Safety System. Back home, I dove into continued development of the Model 551 Microprocessor-Based Controller even as a simmering tension with Lewis, the VP of Engineering, lingered in the background. On the flight home, I thought: one of us would have to go, and I didn't care which one.

During my absence, Preston—a magazine engineer—had unearthed a supposed "golden ticket" in Denver: Zero Systems. Convinced it was CAC's next big break, he'd convinced Lewis and the higher-ups to gamble on an acquisition without truly knowing what they were buying. I was dispatched to evaluate the technical side, only to discover that Zero Systems had little more than a handful of printed circuit boards and a digital tape meant for tank gauging. Their only venture with the digital tape had ended with an oil storage tank explosion.

One crisp evening downtown Denver, I sat with the exuberant VP of Finance over a drink. His eyes shone with anticipation as he rhapsodized about our new venture. I hesitated on the brink of shattering his illusion with the truth.

A few weeks later, with negotiations reaching fever pitch, I joined a final decision meeting. Before that, Bob Howell—a man who cared enough to ask straight questions at lunch—pressed me for my honest opinion. Later, with all eyes fixed on me at the meeting, Charlie leaned in and said, "Bob, tell us what you really think." I laid it out plainly: "It's a bad deal. Every application will need custom software, the packaging won't hold up offshore or in the desert, and we're staring down endless support headaches." There was a heavy pause—a moment that felt like a dropped bomb. Lewis's face went red as I added, "We already have the 551 Controller to meet our needs. Let's stick with what works." I excused myself the tension thick behind me.

Later, Lewis stormed into my office, fury in his eyes and words that stung like icy rain. I shot back, "You don't know what you're doing. Don't ever question my competence!" Despite my warnings, management pressed ahead with the acquisition. Soon enough, Lewis told me I was to be the technical liaison between Zero Systems and CAC. I met this news with a wry, "So, I'm on the team again?"

Within a year and a half, more than a million dollars had been funneled into Zero Systems, and it became painfully evident that Jim C.—one of the original owners—was out of his depth. His lead programmer, who happened to be his girlfriend, could only churn out clunky Fortran code, and during testing their first system on a Gulf platform faltered miserably. About that time, I wrote a confidential letter to Lewis, itemizing how his mismanagement had cost us dearly. He barely skimmed beyond the first page. Later, I passed the letter to Fred Johnson who worked for Charlie.

As if on cue, CAC's new president, Joe B., began making rounds. "Be patient—changes are coming," he had told me in a low, measured tone that both reassured and hinted at upheaval. A week later, Lewis and I flew to Denver, only to find that Joe had already pulled the trigger: he'd hired a consultant, fired Jim C. and his girlfriend, and shuttered Zero Systems. By mid-morning, Lewis was back on a flight to New Orleans with Joe. I was told to wait in the office. later, a call and Lewis's voice broke the news to me: "I've been fired!" The irony wasn't lost on me.

Before long, while I was halfway through a project in Trinidad, CAC decided to relocate operations to Houston. Linda and I sold our New Orleans home and moved to The Woodlands. It wasn't long before a Houston oil company approached CAC with an offshore project. I'd warned against bidding due to the high technical risks, yet a month later, I found my name pinned as the project manager.

In June, while boarding a boat in the churning seas of Trinidad, I slipped. In that moment, the world slowed, and I suspected I might have injured myself—a bilateral inguinal hernia. By September, even though most technical issues were ironed out, the client accused me of a cavalier attitude and delays. CAC handed the reins to Ray O., but I remained at the helm day-to-day.

That summer, corporate reshuffles intensified. The new VP of Engineering, Charles R., and VP of Marketing, Mike R., forced Richard Tullis from his post. On a subsequent trip back to New Orleans, I urged Doug at Petro-xyz to hire Richard, convinced his expertise could open doors—especially with those lucrative Hydraulic Control Panels that once brought in hundreds of thousands per unit.

When the AH project wrapped up, Charles and Ray confronted me, accusing me of taking an unauthorized day off so they could fire me. I calmly advised that I had signed the visitor log at Hewlett-Packard proving otherwise. They missed! I went to my office and in a burst of finality, I emptied all of my files—tossing project data and designs into a dumpster. The next day, I filed an accident report for my hernia, submitted documentation from Trinidad, and scheduled surgery, taking four weeks of sick leave. When I returned, a performance review had dragged my rating from the top tier to the very bottom, and I refused to sign. They promptly relocated me to a back office, hidden away from everyone.

Around that time, my father was fighting his own battle with cancer. I took a vacation to see him in Michigan, but even then, office politics followed: Carol confessed to me later that management had pressured her to lie about my request for additional leave. It wasn't long before the VP of Engineering—the very man trying to manipulate her—was fired by the president.

My father passed away on April 1, and the loss pushed me to resign. I accepted an engineering position with CPU in New Orleans, working on an NOC deepwater platform.

Note: Vernon—the marketing head for a Houston control valve company—quit over a bonus dispute, and his successor Charles R., CAC's fired VP of Engineering lasted three days before succumbing to his deserved fate— fired. Later, the VP of Marketing lost his job when Richard Tullis at Petro-xyz pulled a crucial four-million-dollar order.

NEW ORLEANS COMMUTER

In April 1990, after leaving CAC behind, I decided Houston's tangled freeways were too risky. I started commuting to New Orleans, this time as a contract engineer for CPU on an NOC tension leg platform, working side by side with Ken Callaway—a partner I'd trusted on past projects. Designing the platform's fiber optic network, setting up workstations and Programmable Logic Controllers, and integrating control systems became my new world. I even leased a small apartment near the office, and each weekend, the predictable routine of catching the Thursday afternoon flight from New Orleans offered a bittersweet pause in the relentless grind.

Mr. Chips—my loyal dog—waited in the front window with silent anticipation. His simple joy punctuated the chaos of my professional life, reminding me that solace could be found in the smallest moments. Even as I battled complex engineering challenges, I found comfort in the familiar—the buzz of the early flight, the drive from the airport, and the warmth of returning home.

Between projects on deepwater platforms and designing a supervisory system for an oil production plant in Alabama, the years blurred into long stretches of commutes and deadlines. Evenings sometimes found me sharing beers with friends like Richard Tullis or unwinding with Charlie and Ronnie. I recalled a night aboard Charlie's yacht—an unlikely treasure acquired from a bygone era—drifting on Lake Pontchartrain, the salty air and starlight weaving a temporary reprieve from the pressures of work.

By 1991, I'd moved into a modest room in Metairie. Free moments meant biking quiet neighborhood streets, working out at Curtin's Gym, or savoring wine tastings at Martin's Wine Cellar with Toby Miller, an old friend from my Allen-Bradley days. New Orleans enchanted me with its vibrant food and atmosphere—Liuzza's, with its frosty Coors and golden fried seafood, felt like a small oasis amid my chaotic routine. Weekly dinners with friends on Canal Boulevard and an occasional card game reminded me that life, though unpredictable, could be savored.

At home in Houston, Mr. Chips continued to be my best friend and companion, greeting my every arrival with unspoken joy. Linda—quietly teaching in The Woodlands—kept her routines, even as our lives increasingly diverged. Later, during my years in California, I forged an unexpected friendship with George Nguyen, a Vietnamese fighter pilot who occasionally flew the Houston–New Orleans route for Continental Airlines. Our long talks, shared Texas hold'em games, and even a memorable 21-day Mediterranean cruise with a tight-knit circle of friends, underscored the serendipity of life's connections.

Linda's mischievous cat, Piddy, would often join Mr. Chips in playful tugs at his collar, a small, charming reminder that even in the midst of turmoil, moments of lightness could still be found.

Looking back, engineering meetings, design reviews and occasional confrontations, to quiet rides home and shared smiles with my faithful dog—wove together into a tapestry of struggle, loss, and unexpected grace. Each moment, whether bitter or sweet, left an indelible mark, subtly foreshadowing the changes that ultimately carried me forward into a new chapter.

PETRO-XYZ: THE EARLY YEARS WITH BILL, DOUG, AND TERRY

Bill and Doug founded Petro-xyz with a good business plan but required Terry for technical backup when they were away. They recruited many experienced personnel from CAC's shop and office staff with no opposition from CAC's president.

Bill, a Texas A&M graduate in Mechanical Engineering, was not bound by conventional thinking. Doug was a graduate from Princeton with a master's degree in electrical engineering. Bill was the one you never wanted to cross. He was principled with a reputation built on action that left little room for debate.

In 1974, when CAC's Belle Chasse telephone line was plagued by a stubborn fault, Bill tired of endless calls to the phone company. One day, he decided to take care of the problem himself and sent 460 volts of AC power to a remote junction box. The phone company fumed over the burned wiring. When they demanded answers, Bill's calm reply was: **"I told you to fix it."**

At his cabin downriver in the delta marshlands, repeated thefts of his boat batteries had started to wear on him. Bill's solution was as inventive as it was ruthless, a modified battery that sent a clear message. No more battery theft.

Doug should have known better but pushed Bill over a serious business disagreement. Saturday morning in Covington, he unlocked his airplane cockpit only to find a small note taped to the seat: **"Have a nice flight.– Bill."**

Doug taxied the aircraft around the field but would not take off. Back across the lake, Doug confronted Bill. All Bill offered was a quiet smile. Doug never challenged him again.

SOUTHERN LOUISIANA PROBLEM-SOLVING

Out in Southern Louisiana, disputes were settled with a mix of local savvy and unexpected tactics. Maurice, a Cajun friend from Arcadia, had grown tired of his sister's boyfriend ignoring warnings. One day, the stubborn man found himself in his pickup with a cottonmouth snake biting him—a painful lesson rendered in nature's own harsh tongue. Later, Maurice visited him and said, half-smirking, "Man, I'm real sorry someone did something like that to you." The message was clear: respect was not optional.

JOINING PETRO-XYZ

The summer of 1991 marked a turning point. Dorsey, a reserved but shrewd former Texaco project manager now managing Petro-xyz's contract services, called me in for an interview. Soon after, I found myself deep in the grind—working as a contract engineer on gas compressor modules for NOC's deep-water platforms, split between New Orleans and Houston with a relentless Monday-to-Thursday schedule.

Each compressor module was a marvel of self-contained engineering—a maze of control valves, safety systems, and automated sequencing that took over a year to design through commissioning. Nearing completion, under the flickering lights of the construction yard, Norris, NOC's project manager, and I meticulously tested every system until nothing left the site, unless it could stand up to the challenge.

MENTORING AND LESSONS LEARNED

In the bustle of Petro-xyz's early days, I mentored a young engineer, Steve Ronan, whose eager eyes and steady hand eventually carried my torch at Hydril when I later stepped away after losing Linda.

Living in New Orleans meant always staying on alert. I still remember one early, morning at 5 a.m. leaving a grocery store when I noticed a car tailing me—a subtle but unmistakable threat of a carjack. I steered onto a long, dim driveway leading to a nursing home. The car passed me by, vanishing into the shadows of a nearby housing project, leaving me in the silent streets.

Later, relatives from Crown Point would confess that even in broad daylight, the streets had turned perilous—with handguns a common sight on every corner.

By April 1999, as oil prices tumbled to $10 a barrel, my chapter with Petro-xyz closed. I headed back to Houston with a head full of memories—of bold actions, unspoken warnings, and a restless energy.

HOUSTON RESTART

It was June 1999 when I first spotted the Hydril ad in the Sunday classifieds—a small notice promising a new beginning near the airport. I e-mailed in my resume and soon, Mark Zimmer called. His warm, yet brisk voice set the tone during our interview the very next day. "Ever worked with Louis from CAC?" he asked casually. I replied, "Yeah, I did." Mark leaned in with a wry smile. "He barely lasted a few weeks here—he had a habit of threatening to fire people." That endorsement was enough for me to sign on.

A year later, after Mark's departure, I found myself stepping into a broader role. Suddenly, I was overseeing everything from hydraulic and electrical systems to fiber optic cabling for deepwater Blowout Preventers operating thousands of feet below. I partnered closely with Richard Davidson on subsea computers and software, and even hired Miguel Timm on contract. When Linda passed away four years later, I knew it was time for change, and eventually, Steve Ronan stepped into my shoes.

At Hydril, every project felt like an expedition. I engineered systems on drill ships in Norway—with long, cold nights in Bergen, where I discovered a strange comfort in Hansa Beer and pickled herring—and in Canada braved Edmonton's biting winter on surface control projects. One commissioning trip in Norway became unforgettable. Upper management sent a young engineer eager to soak up as much experience as he could. As we wrapped up, we caught a flight to Amsterdam. Over dinner near the train station and a stroll through a canal lined with neon and mystery, I urged him, "Stay a couple more days. Let yourself absorb this city." His hesitant smile said enough. But when I later returned to a busy coffeehouse, his absence was a quiet reminder that our paths had already begun to diverge.

Things took a sharp turn in July 2002 when Linda was diagnosed with small cell lung cancer. I scaled back to part-time work, supervising Miguel and Steve. When Linda passed away the following April, I retired from Hydril—a decision heavy with both loss and relief.

The next year, alongside Miguel, I co-founded Axion Technology. In those years, I shared laughter and long talks with DeLinda. When she, too, succumbed to lung cancer, I found myself pulled back into engineering with EDG, working under Leroy Cook—an old friend from my New Orleans commuting days. By then, I had handed over my old house to my daughter Andrea and moved into a modest apartment near Westheimer and Beltway 8.

Work at EDG eventually slowed, and on my final day, I sat cross-legged on my apartment floor, sorting through old drawings and quietly wondering about my next move. The phone rang, shattering the stillness. It was Paul Hickey from Solar Turbines, asking if I could work on Mars 15,000 HP packages for PEMEX and Petrobras. I agreed immediately, and the next day, I was back at it—this time with a new partner by my side, Linh. Soon enough, our lives became a constant balance of Houston, Alabama, and California, surrounded by energetic, ambitious young people and the promise of something new.

CALIFORNIA LIVING

In January 2016, Linh and I relocated to Riverside, settling into the upstairs area of Quynh's spacious home—a separate world of 1,400 square feet where the light fell just right across a cozy bedroom and expansive living area. Half of our Alabama furnishings found a new home here, while the rest were carefully stored away. We shared the main-floor kitchen with Quynh and her husband, Jimmy, whose easy hospitality and frequent weekend parties introduced us to a lively group of Vietnamese friends from Bolsa and Westminster.

One April, as we sailed from Venice to Spain with George, Jackie, and several others, the boundaries between work and pleasure blurred. Nights of Texas hold'em poker, punctuated by laughter over glasses of champagne and quiet boasts about a hand featuring four deuces, became a ritual. Linh reconnected with old friends from Vietnam and California, sharing bittersweet stories about her father—a South Vietnamese colonel whose life was forever altered by the fall of Saigon and years in prison.

Living with Quynh and Jimmy opened unexpected doors. I became a full-time grandfather and tutor to Chloe during her elementary years. Mornings began with her excited chatter as we drove to school, afternoons melted into study, trips to the park, swimming, and visits to local attractions. Those three years were transformative—a blend of routine and wonder that I'll always hold close.

Not all encounters were gentle. I recall a dinner at Jim and Lorrie's in Alta Loma. We sat down only to watch as an electrical fire erupted in the kitchen oven and firefighters rushed in. Later, a quiet evening in Jim's den took a dangerous turn when he casually displayed his loaded.22 pistol. A blank moment and a misjudged trigger pull sent a stray bullet ricocheting past Lorrie. After that, I found myself opting for their company only in restaurants and coffee shops, thinking I had bad karma.

After a few family disagreements, Linh and I eventually moved back to Foley, embracing the slow rhythm of a cozy home, tending a garden, and facing new health challenges with the same quiet determination that had carried us this far.

Each chapter felt like a new restart—a blend of unexpected calls, swift goodbyes, and the relentless hope that every ending whispered the promise of another beginning.

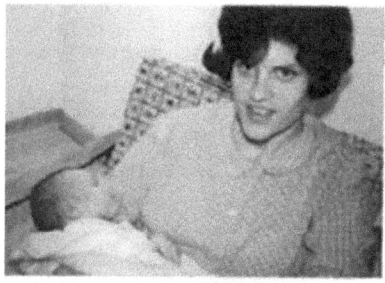

Linda: 1965 Andrea and Linda– 1946 Miles & Linda

Late 1980s: Bob & Linda (Deutsches
Haus N.O.)– Holly Cross Party

Early 1990s: Andrea & Daniel

Brunei 1976: APC-6, Lex's Home,
South China Sea & Mickey

Compressor Modules 1999– West Bank New Orleans

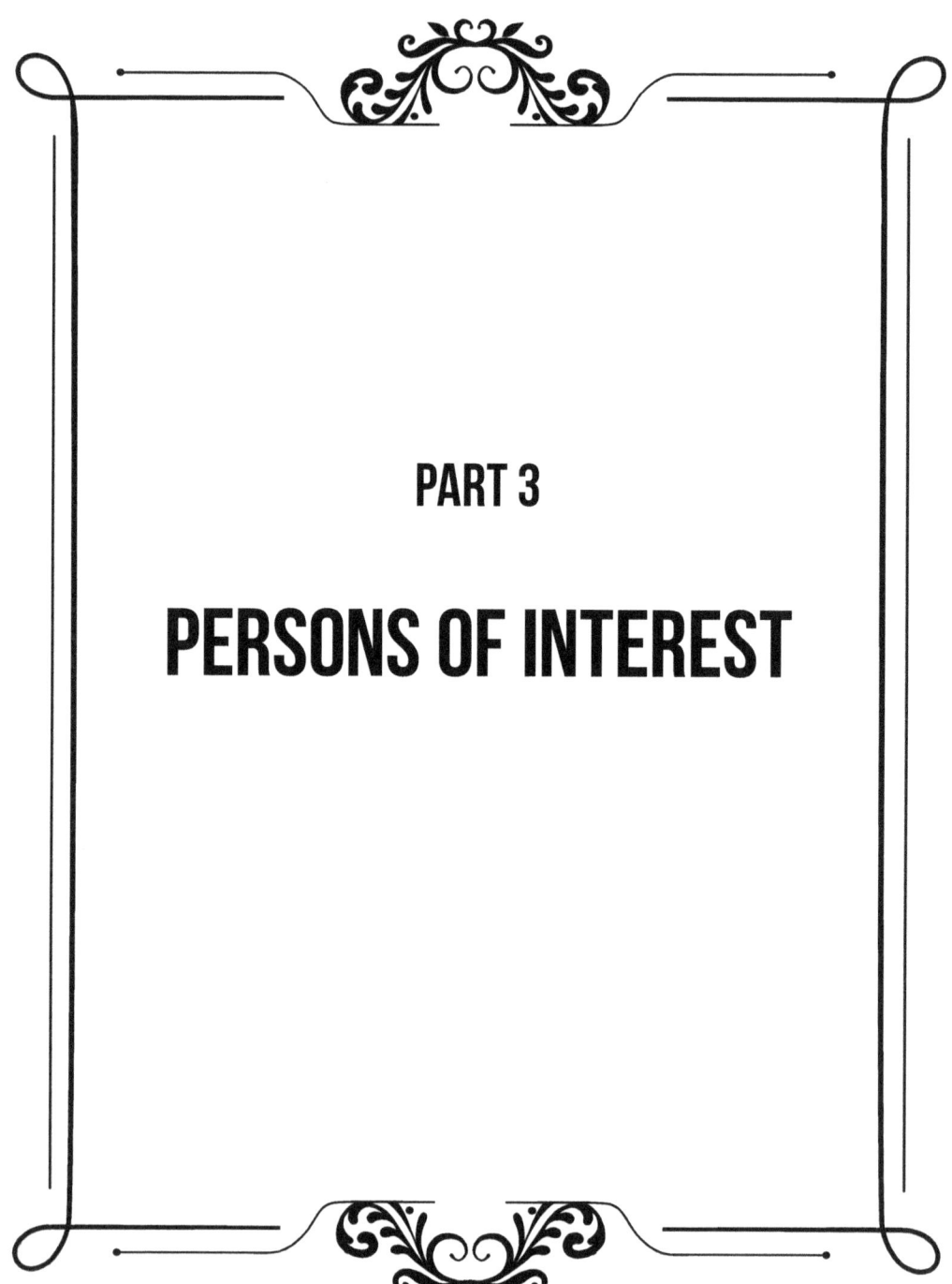

PART 3

PERSONS OF INTEREST

WALLY

"Higher, Bobby Higher!"

I was almost seven, walking home on a bright May Sunday morning in 1944 after Mass at St. Luke's. The familiar path along Joy Road Avenue led me past Herbie's Shoe Repair Shop—a cozy little world of worn leather and the steady clack of sewing machines. My mother often sent me there to have her shoes mended, and I'd sit quietly, absorbing the rich scent of shoe polish and oil as Herbie worked with calloused hands behind the long counter.

That morning, something caught my eye in the alley behind the shop: a small pile of discarded cobbler's shoe stands. In a burst of childish impulsiveness, I scooped up two battered stands and began tossing them along the concrete alleyway on my way home. After a short distance, I discarded one but kept throwing the remaining one toward our house. At the back fence, I could hear Wally from the upstairs window, urging, "Higher, Bobby Higher!" as the stand arced through the air. I kept one arm raised over my head, unwilling to look up to meet it flight. Suddenly—it came down on my head. Pain and shock mingled as I saw my warm blood run down onto my white shirt. I bolted to the back door, calling out for my father, who rushed out with concern etched in his face. Later, the local druggist carefully cleaned and bandaged my wound.

Over time, my father would listen to Wally's endless plans and schemes, involving a mix of daring ideas and playful pranks. I loved Wally, my big brother, and became his personal valet, fetching ice cream or cigarettes for him and even sometimes skipping church just to be in his wake. Those days were alive with laughter, daring, and lessons learned on the fly. There were also warnings from my father, "Higher, Bobby Higher!"

HOT ROD

Summer arrived in a swirl of anticipation. My dad had just ordered a new 1948 Pontiac, a green four-door sedan with brown trim and sold Wally his 1935 Ford. Wally, now old enough and thirsty for freedom, was granted his driver's license. Wally had always loved a good thrill, especially when it came to pushing limits. He'd modify the Ford for speed, and continue power shifting along Livernois Avenue, as if he were a race car driver at the Motor City Speedway!

Until the delivery of the Pontiac, my father was still driving the Ford to work. One early morning, dad and I set off for work in the dim pre-dawn light. Dad fumbled around for the long gear shift lever—only to discover it had been shortened by Wally, complete with a new racing ball knob. Exasperated, he said to himself, "What did you do, Wally?" During the drive, dad grumbled and cursed at each traffic light as he shifted the gears with the short cutoff lever. I couldn't help but smile at the absurdity. Even though dad's annoyance was palpable, it was clear that Wally's mischief was part of a larger, unspoken promise of rebellion—a hint at adventures yet to come.

CIGARETTE MONEY, 1948

Cigarettes were cheap then, but at eighteen, there were other things to spend money on, and a shortage of funds was all too likely. Wally had just finished high school and started a job with the U.S. Postal Service, driving a truck to pick up and deliver mail and parcels. In the summertime, he began work around 7:30 a.m. and was usually home by about 5:00 p.m.

Occasionally, he would go through the letters looking for money—picking up a few dollars here and there to support his smoking habit. One day, he noticed a box from a jeweler in New York addressed to a local jewelry shop and set it aside until later. During his lunch break, he opened the box to discover about thirty diamond rings. Stunned, he wondered what to do next. Realizing this was grand theft, he spent a day or two agonizing over how to dispose of them. Believing he couldn't reseal the box unnoticed to make the delivery, he decided instead to bury the rings in a spot where he would not be tempted to dig them up and try to sell them. There was a new Heinz 57 garage being built near the corner of Joy Road and Livernois, across the railroad tracks; the rebar for the garage floor was finished and ready for the concrete. That night, he buried the rings. Later, driving by the completed garage with its concrete floor, he felt more at ease, putting the rings firmly in his past.

The postal inspectors never approached Wally directly about the missing box of rings, though they suspected he was the last person to have handled the package. A few weeks later, Wally noticed a partially opened letter with a few dollars sticking out—cigarette money. He placed the money in his wallet and set the letter aside. That afternoon, when he returned to the postal garage to park the truck, postal inspectors were waiting and asked him for the letter. The letter was in the truck, but the money was missing.

The next morning, Wally left for work as usual. Later, my mother picked up the morning newspaper with her coffee. Several pages in, she began reading:

"Walter V. Furmaga was arrested and arraigned before the First Federal District Court in Detroit, Michigan on charges of mail theft."

She screamed in shock at the same time her neighbor Violet called to tell Sylvia about Wally's arrest. His years of petty theft had finally caught up with him. Weeks later, at trial, Wally was sentenced to serve probation for five years, reporting to the probation office as scheduled. He might never have been caught if not for the cigarette money.

Each of these moments, from the careless toss of a shoe stand to the reckless modifications of a car's gear shift lever, and even the desperate act of hiding stolen rings, wove together the fabric of our youth. They were punctuated by laughter, exasperated glances, and the silent acknowledgment that every misadventure carried with it a lesson—one that hinted at the unpredictable roads we were all destined to travel.

A NEW HOME

Years before the war, my father had wanted to buy a new home in the northwest area of Detroit near Greenfield and Six Mile Roads, but he could not raise the money for a down payment. Now, in the late spring of 1950, his dream had become a reality—16596 Coyle. I had just finished the seventh grade at Sherrill and would work with him on repainting all the rooms and closets (my job, armed with a small two-inch paintbrush, was to learn how to paint closets), sanding and varnishing the floors, installing new light fixtures, carpeting, remodeling the kitchen, and handling numerous outdoor tasks—including repainting the exterior trim—before our move-in scheduled for early August.

My father spared no expense in getting the house exactly right—new living room furniture, bedroom outfits, a refinished dining room set, a new electric stove, refrigerator, and kitchen dining set. He loved the fireplace mantel, selecting a clock that chimed on the hour, and paid special attention to choosing the fireplace tools.

The Korean War had started in June, and both my brothers, Wally and Gerry, were up for the draft. Gerry would leave in November, and Wally is another story. My sister Rosemary was now planning a wedding for January. It was a five-bedroom house, and in a brief time, most of my siblings would be gone. We moved in, and it was time for me to start at a new school. Wally was working at the Dodge Plant during the day, carousing at night, and customizing his 1940 Pontiac Club Coupe whenever he had a few bucks. I don't think we were in the house more than a week or two when my parents were out and Rosemary and Gerry were working. Wally was in the living room on the sofa, and I was busy in the kitchen fixing a snack. The next thing I heard was Wally shouting. He had fallen asleep on the sofa while smoking a cigarette, which had fallen between the cushions, and the sofa was on fire and smoking. There was a faucet and a garden hose on the side of the house near the front door. Wally ran out the front door, turned on the water, and ran back with the hose still on—extinguishing the fire and soaking the entryway and living room carpet. The fire was out!

He then got me to help him clean up the mess by soaking up some of the water from the carpet with bath towels and covering up the surface damage to the sofa as if no one would notice. By the time we finished, everything looked good!

It was not long before my parents parked in the driveway and entered through the front door. My mother screamed "Walter," along with some other words in Polish, as she stepped onto the water-soaked carpet with extra-thick matting, making a squishing sound as she walked into the room. By then, my father was in the living room, trying to grasp what was happening. I don't remember all the details that followed, but Wally concocted a plausible story—full of half-truths—as to how the sofa caught fire! Later, there were insurance claims for the sofa, smoke, and water damage. Wally would explain to my parents how they had made money on the fire, taking a little credit for their windfall. What you must admire about Wally was his ability to slightly alter the facts in any situation to minimize any responsibility he might have had.

THE DRAFT

The Korean War was underway, and Wally had received his draft notice to report for induction into the armed services—Fort Wayne! While working at the Dodge Truck Plant, his hands frequently came into contact with the oil and chemicals used in assembling the trucks. As a result, he developed a skin rash on both hands—ugly bumps and small blisters.

On the scheduled induction date, Wally reported to Fort Wayne and went through the standard process, which included a complete physical. A doctor noted his skin condition and informed him that his induction would be delayed until the rash cleared. He was temporarily classified as 4E.

At first, Wally was slightly disappointed by the rejection, but as the war escalated and most eligible men aged 18 to 26 were drafted, he soon discovered an unexpected silver lining—there were plenty of young women wherever he went. Whether at bars, dances, or summer lake gatherings, he and his buddy, Jimmy Sikes (classified 4F), enjoyed their newfound social advantage.

Still employed at the Dodge Plant, Wally made sure to keep a bottle of the plant's oil concoction in his bedroom. Every few days, he would rub the oil on his hands to keep the rash active. This went on for about two years. Approximately eight months later, he was recalled for another medical evaluation but managed to maintain his rash and 4E classification. He was never called for induction again.

WINTER WONDERLAND

He customized a 1940 Pontiac until it gleamed beautifully in the afternoon sun—then totaled it after a wedding and too much to drink. Unemployment checks and a neighbor's part-time delivery route kept him solvent, but the replacement car, a'41 Buick with failing brakes, turned every errand into a carnival ride.

One January afternoon, snow piled high along Puritan Avenue. Wally craved cigarettes. We crawled down the street at ten miles an hour, doors open, boots scraping the snow and ice, whenever he needed to "brake." The city felt abandoned—no patrol cars, just the crunch of our tires and the sound of the old Buick's engine. Back home, we laughed ourselves breathless, but a shiver slid down my spine: sooner or later, the brakes—or the luck—would fail.

SUMMER AND A NEW LIFE

It was time for Wally to leave the Dodge Truck Plant. Growing up, our father was a milkman, delivering milk in the 1930s with a horse-drawn wagon. After the war, he switched to a Divco truck. Wally, Gerry, and I often worked as "jumpers," helping him deliver milk to homes along his route in Hamtramck.

For Wally, transitioning from the truck plant to Sealtest Dairy was easy. Initially, he worked as a swingman, covering for other drivers on their days off and vacations. Eventually, he was assigned a permanent route on Grosse Ile. Each morning, around 6:30 a.m., his truck would already be loaded with milk and ice when he arrived at work. Within a week or two, he memorized his route and became remarkably efficient—typically finishing his deliveries by 10:30 a.m.

I worked with him as a jumper a few times when our father was off. Even when working alone, Wally was so fast that his coworkers nicknamed him "Flash." Most days, he was on his way home well before noon. Occasionally, he'd meet our uncle Ziggy, who also worked as a milkman for the same dairy, for a beer and a hamburger at a nearby tavern.

As summer faded into fall, Wally moved on. He took a new job driving a truck for Kool Vent Awnings, a company that manufactured ammunition boxes for the Detroit Tank Arsenal. Every afternoon, he made deliveries to the arsenal—a 30- to 40-mile drive one way. He quickly figured out how to maximize his time; often, he'd delay his return, padding his time sheet with extra overtime hours. I went along with him a few times. On one occasion, the office called the arsenal to check on him. Fortunately for Wally, he happened to be there at that moment and told them he was "waiting to be unloaded." In reality, his truck had already been emptied, and he was just killing time.

By late 1953, tank production was slowing, and Wally took another job with a furniture company, delivering appliances. As his marriage approached, Wally began to consider a serious career. He had studied machine shop and drafting at Wilbur Wright Trade School from ages 15 to 17, and his experience at the Dodge Truck Plant gave him valuable insight into automotive manufacturing.

Taking a pay cut, he started as a detailer for an engineering company that specialized in die design for auto manufacturing. This decision set him on a path that would eventually lead to his own company, airplanes, luxury cars, and a lavish lifestyle—far beyond anything he had imagined growing up. But was it all a success? There was a price to pay, influenced by money, character, ego, genetics—and the eventual end of his good luck.

A NOTE ABOUT WALLY'S ENGINEERING SKILLS

After a few years in business, Wally felt uneasy about his lack of formal engineering credentials when dealing with client engineering staff. He asked me if I thought he should go back to school for an engineering degree. I told him, "Walt, you already know more about engineering design, automotive manufacturing, and business than you'll ever learn in college. You want a degree? Hire one!"

BID OR GET OUT

This was his favorite poker game, played monthly on Friday nights with a group of friends and business associates. Occasionally, a new face would join the game, invited by one of his friends. In Bid or Get Out, if you believed you had the best hand, you kept bidding until all the other players dropped out.

One Friday night, a new player appeared—Nadel. It was around 1980, and I was working in New Orleans, doing engineering work on gas turbine compressor packages for offshore production facilities in the Gulf. Wally called me about investing in oil leases in Alaska. He explained that the investment was structured like Bid or Get Out—a $20,000 buy-in to play. I told him that bringing leases to production required years of work and significant capital—for drilling, production equipment, power services, and pipelines. I left the decision up to him.

A few years passed, and he confided that he had over a million dollars invested in the leases. Nadel was pushing him for even more money. They were supposedly getting close to selling the leases.

"Walt, did you ever check this guy out?" I asked.

More time went by, and Walt told me he had purchased $400,000 worth of Gordian gold coins through Nadel. I suggested he take one of the coins to get it appraised and authenticated, but he never followed up on my advice.

Sometime later, he called me again. This time, he needed a check for $5,000 to give to Nadel—to convince him he was receiving money from relatives to invest in the leases. The leases were supposed to be sold within a few months, and Walt assured me I'd receive $150,000 from the sale. If anything went wrong, I was not to mention the $5,000 or the loss.

Not long after, Wally received a call from the FBI. Nadel had been arrested for running a confidence scam, swindling seven other people—just like Wally—out of millions. A few weeks later, Wally called again. He had gotten Nadel in trouble with the judge for discussing the arrest and trial with him.

I told Walt, "Nadel will do a year or two in prison, get paroled, and then take off for the Riviera with the swindle money in a Swiss bank."

Walt never mentioned my $5,000. I was so furious that I didn't speak to him for weeks. I even wrote him a letter about how he had made me part of his failure—but I never sent it.

Again, "Higher, Bobby Higher!"

RUNNING OUT OF LUCK

Wally had always been lucky, but now the patterns in his lifestyle were catching up to him. In his early seventies, he had been a heavy smoker since his teenage years, averaging at least two packs of Lucky Strikes per day. He loved doughnuts, rich food, and more than an occasional cocktail. Exercise had never been a priority.

A routine flight physical uncovered some health concerns. The initial test results weren't good. If he wanted to enjoy his retirement years, he would need medical intervention. His heart, lungs, and prostate were showing signs of aging and years of abuse. His heart was the primary concern, and the flight physician recommended that he see a specialist for further testing.

Walt visited a cardiologist for a full battery of diagnostic tests. The results led to a recommendation for an angioplasty with a stent to widen his partially blocked arteries. The doctor explained the risks—about three percent of patients experience postsurgical complications. Without the procedure, his quality of life would steadily decline. Walt decided to take the risk.

As he put on his hospital gown for the procedure, he reflected on how he had avoided surgeries throughout his life. Now, he had no choice but to go through with what seemed like a relatively low-risk procedure. No one expected anything life-threatening. He had always managed to come through tight situations—with luck on his side.

The surgeon viewed this as a routine case. He was scheduled to leave the next day for a short vacation in the Bahamas. It was early November in Michigan, and two light snowfalls had already come and gone. As he worked the surgical probe through Walt's arteries—something he had done countless times before—he noted an excessive amount of plaque obstructing the probe's path. Despite this, he completed the procedure without further concern.

Walt was moved to recovery, and the surgeon went to update the family. He assured them the procedure had gone well and recommended a follow-up visit in two weeks, after his return from vacation. In the meantime, his associate would monitor Walt's recovery, and he was expected to go home the following day.

That night and into the next morning, Walt wasn't feeling well. He didn't realize that the procedure had dislodged plaque, which was now blocking blood flow to his intestine—causing the tissue to die. This condition, known as intestinal ischemia, was developing unnoticed.

His son, who worked in medical research, alerted the associate to Walt's worsening condition, but there was no significant response. Days passed. Walt's discomfort intensified. His condition was becoming terminal. Just before Thanksgiving, he left for his condominium in Florida.

I visited him in mid-January. He had quit smoking, and eating was becoming increasingly difficult. Walt passed away in early April.

CODA

At the funeral I remembered Wally hosing down a burning sofa, hands slick with assembly-line oil, and cards shuffled at the poker table. Luck, it turned out, was a finite resource—spent a dollar at a time, a mile, a cigarette, a bluff. But for a while, my brother lived as though the deck would never run out. Later, on quiet nights, I thought I could hear that old clock strike and half expect Wally to shout from the other room, "Higher, Bobby—Higher!"

THE FAMILY TRUST

Walt had amassed over six million dollars by the time he decided to set up a family trust. He trusted only those who danced on the edge of legality—a quality perfectly embodied by the lawyer he'd known for years, a man who handled both his legal and business affairs with a certain nonchalance.

I remember that brisk afternoon when Walt introduced me to the lawyer over lunch. He never mentioned that his eldest son and I would later serve as administrators for the trust. Walt preferred a slow drip of details; he revealed only what was necessary. I'd long suspected he'd once borrowed my engineering license to bolster the credentials of his company, Diemation Engineering—a little secret he kept to himself despite its clear illegality.

Wally and Alice, his children, bore the unmistakable marks of his influence. Wally had special talents in die-design and marketing and was unafraid to cut corners or bend rules if it meant outsmarting a competitor. His success was measured not in ethics but in bold, cold cash. In his shadow, his daughter and youngest son learned to navigate a world where the ends always justified the means.

The youngest son, however, was a force of self-destruction. Since childhood, he'd been tangled in drugs and petty theft—rifling through their neighbors' personal belongings, while a guest in their home, and even snatching purses. His reckless path led to repeated run-ins with the law, car wrecks that left fourteen cars damaged in his wake, and payoffs from Wally that barely kept him out of jail. Eventually, the man who had spiraled through countless crimes succumbed quietly to sleep apnea one bitter night.

In contrast, the oldest son had chosen a steadier road—a career in medical research, built on convention, a marriage that promised stability, and two daughters raised with careful love. His path was a silent counterpoint to the chaos that had engulfed the rest of us.

After Walt passed, the trust's fortune ignited old family tensions. Alice, suddenly free to spend without restraint, began modestly with a used car. But that modesty was short-lived—a blue Jaguar convertible, a dashing New York boyfriend, sparkling jewels, and an opulent lifestyle followed. Before long, with cunning assistance from her daughter and that ever-resourceful lawyer, she had rapidly drained the trust. I was eventually asked by the eldest son to draft a letter to a judge, detailing the quiet, relentless dismantling of Walt's legacy. In the end, control of both the trust and Alice's personal funds slipped into the eldest son's hands. A stroke left Alice vulnerable until her own son intervened, rescuing her from the prospects of a bleak nursing home. Meanwhile, the New York boyfriend vanished like the money.

The cascade of misfortune continued: her daughter and son-in-law eventually landed in a Florida prison under shadowy charges—drugs, bad checks, forgery—none of which could quiet the whispers of scandal. Their son, crushed by despair and suffocated by family failure, ended his life one dismal Friday in the basement of her townhouse; his still form was only discovered Monday morning by the housekeeper.

I still recall the surreal phone call during Hurricane Katrina. While the storm raged, Alice was on the line, her words rang out with venom, "It's all that Black mayor's fault!" The call transported me back to bitter moments—the sting of Wally's mocking "Airhead!" echoing in my ears. Out of equal parts frustration and a desperate need to ground us in truth, I sent her a letter detailing Walt's past escapades. Months passed without response until one day the envelope returned, marked simply "Undeliverable." I held it, as though it was a silent warning that some secrets might be better left buried. No sooner had I set it aside than new scandals unfurled: once again, her youngest son was arrested in Livonia, and it wasn't long before her daughter and son-in-law were off to serve time.

Each twist of fate in our family felt inevitable—a relentless cycle of ambition, betrayal, and sorrow that promised more chapters of turmoil lurking just beyond the horizon.

GERRY

No Concessions

He was born on a cold November day—the tenth—in 1931. From birth, he suffered from a membrane blockage in his stomach that prevented him from receiving nourishment. After several days, my parents took him to Dr. Watson, who prescribed lactic acid to break through the membrane. It was successful, but it was a difficult experience for the infant. I have always wondered whether he suffered any mental damage from that metabolic ordeal.

As Gerry grew up, he began to understand the power of authority. Walter, our father, attempted to break Gerry's will and bend him into submission. To what extent? That is debatable. As a result, Gerry became defiant. Catholic school only reinforced his resistance, twisting his mind with religious dogma, conformity, and the suppression of free will.

It had all started well enough. The Korean War had ended, and Gerry was in his final year of college when he met Barbara at a friend's wedding. A courtship followed, but there was a darkness within him—a need for control—that she did not see. Throughout his youth, he had learned to suppress and conceal this trait, deceiving others and even himself. He believed he was a good altar boy, and believed that the beatings he had endured from his father had forged the strong, dominant character essential to manhood.

Once they married, there was no longer any need to hide the scars of his past. She was his—for life. In the home, Gerry became a devout Catholic, ensuring that his wife and children attended Mass every Sunday—sometimes even on weekdays. His son, Kenny, struggled with alcohol and drugs to numb his life's problems, and Gerry believed that rigid religious discipline could correct him. At church, Gerry organized Sunday breakfasts and bizarre fundraisers.

There was no obvious trait or signs of a personality disorder, but there was a subtle control he exercised in his environment and relationships.

Early in their marriage, they had sought counseling from a priest. But with five children under six, the best advice he could offer was for them to "live as brother and sister"—a stock response from the church. She could submit to his demands, or she could choose abstinence. Either way, the emotional toll was too high.

Barbara had entertained early thoughts of leaving, but she had missed her chance. Frequent pregnancies and financial dependence trapped her; she told herself there would be time later—after the children were grown. Gerry's controlling nature and sexual demands weighed heavily on Barbara, eventually driving her to abuse alcohol. Barbara was always a devoted mother to their children, who also suffered under his oppressive rule, leaving them emotionally scarred well into adulthood.

Gerry spent his career in the data processing department of an auto manufacturer, but his confrontational attitude and social difficulties with management led to constant battles over issues on which he disagreed. This ultimately resulted in his early retirement at fifty.

THE LAST VISIT— NOVEMBER 2018

I remember visiting him fifteen years earlier. The vibrant runner who had once raced the wind in high school was now a heavyset man, burdened by arthritis and memories of battles fought—both in the office and at home.

Their fiftieth wedding anniversary had been arranged by their five children. The event passed in silence, save for a few forced words between them. Neither had wanted to be there or to be reminded of the years lost to unhappiness.

Now, Barbara was gone. His eldest son, Kenny, was dead, claimed by drugs and alcohol. The family structure had further crumbled, with the remaining children alienated and Gerry rejecting all attempts by them to help him.

Gerry would spend his final days isolated in a group home for mentally impaired adults, suffering from advanced dementia.

Gerry's life was a tapestry of battles fought and lost, of control wielded and ultimately crumbling. Throughout his life, he never offered any concessions, it was not in his nature. He was obstinate and resolute in his convictions. In the end with his mind impaired by dementia and with a further withdraw from his reality, there was only a blank stare that remained at death.

Through most of those married years, I would spend time on the telephone and during visits to Michigan, trying to reach his mind in hopes of his seeing what he was doing to the people in his life, but to no avail. I really did love him, but like most, I finally gave up!

LILLIAN

Our first year on Coyle Avenue, my parents became friends with Ann and Maury across the street with Lillian and Mark, their next-door neighbors. Mark hired me to shovel snow off the sidewalk throughout the winter and during the warm months cut his lawn. My dad told me that Maury was a bag man for a judge but worked as a union leader in one of the auto plants. I was hit by the flu in the winter of 1951, missing two weeks of school. Maury helped me clear my sinus by suggesting I eat a raw onion which for some reason only worked once. The following spring, Mark died from colon cancer and Lillian was alone, attractive and in her early forties.

By the Fall of 1952, the Korean War was ending, and Gerry was out of the Army and living at home for a while. Soon, he started an affair with Lillian, and they were not discrete. Ann would call my mother relating some of the details, observed through the windows which was becoming a neighborhood scandal. Gerry moved out but kept seeing her, parking in the alley behind her garage. One time my mother was at the bus stop on Six-Mile Road, and a strange woman started a conversation about the scandal, not realizing that Gerry was my mother's son. No peace for Sylvia.

The affair finally ended, but every time my mother left the house and looked across the street, she would get upset. Months passed, and my parents bought a new home on Norfolk Avenue, off Telegraph Road and moved. I never talked to Lillian again after Gerry's started the affair and Lillian grew to hate my mother for the scandal. Before we moved, I passed Lillian walking the other way across the street, she gave me a very strange look …

ROSEMARY

For as long as I can remember, I've wrestled with understanding my sister Rosemary. I've penned thoughts on her behavior around the family, but now I find myself wondering—what kind of person was she really? And do any of these reflections still matter?

My mother and Aunt Clara always described her as tender and selfless—a warm presence in every environment, a whiz in the kitchen, and a pleasant reliable factor in our early home. I recall the aroma of her cooking mingling with the soft hum of weekend chatter, the quiet pride in a well-kept home. Yet beneath that picture of domestic perfection, I suspect old wounds, and misdirected lessons had taken root.

Rosemary's path was set early. Leaving high school in the tenth grade to work at Woolworth's, she married Richard in January 1951 and later clocked extra hours at the Bell Telephone Company before little Jerry started school. Even then, she followed the script handed down by our mother—Rosemary would be a homemaker with little thought of another life, with heaps of advice from Walter and Sylvia. Their words, good or not, were a constant undercurrent in her marriage, painting love with streaks of tension and expectation.

On Greenview, life was a collage of bright summers and quirky mishaps. I remember the weekends at the Daysons' cottage at Cass Lake—the echoing laughter of the Dayson boys and Eddie Wallick, and Richard tirelessly working on home projects. He built a brick wall behind the TV, revamped the porch, and even erected a fence that seemed as stubborn as Rosemary herself. Their dog, Shooter, with clumsy, oversized paws, quickly earned a reputation for sneaking treats from the kitchen table, his antics as unpredictable as summer storms. One afternoon, a broken pool wall sent a three-foot surge of water crashing into Harold's basement, and even that disaster could never dampen the spirit of the neighborhood gatherings.

I spent many evenings under the same roof, babysitting. Richard would drive me home, our conversations about school, life and plans for the future, flowing easily.

But as the years slipped by, the gap between Rosemary and Richard grew wider. While he chased further education and a career in medicine and academia, she clung to the traditions of her youth. When Richard finally left, it wasn't just his presence that vanished—it was the dream they'd once built together. Left to raise Jerry and step into the unforgiving world of business, she carried both love and a lingering guilt over their failure.

In her new battles, the echoes of our father, Walter, seemed never far away. Navigating the office at a liquor distributor, felt like a replay of childhood skirmishes, each encounter with men stirring memories of past conquests and bruised pride. I remember her snapping over a seemingly trivial dinner arrangement one evening, the firmness in her tone belying years of unspoken hurt. In those moments, she reminded me of Aunt Joan—a reflection of a fierce spirit armed with a chip on her shoulder and an unwavering desire to control her fate.

Time, however, has its own way of softening edges. After a string of troubled relationships, Rosemary found an unexpected steadiness with Stuart. Though their love was quieter than what she'd known with Richard, Stuart's steady presence allowed her to reclaim pieces of the dream she once had—a dream of simple joy, of a home filled not only with routine but with genuine connection. Even so, her need to set every dinner plan or dictate the itinerary for family trips hinted at unfinished battles with her past.

Now, as I sift through old memories and faded photographs, I see Rosemary as a mosaic of early hopes and later defiance. In her meticulously scheduled life, unexpected moments—like the soft rustle of an evening breeze through an open window or the spontaneous burst of laughter over a card game or puzzle—that beneath all the control, a fragile hope lingers, hinting at a future where even the most well-ordered life might learn to bend without breaking.

RICHARD

Sometimes life offers a person who reshapes your world without fanfare. I was twelve when my sister Rosemary started dating Richard Dudek—a young man whose weathered eyes hinted at battles fought long before his twenties. His early years had been molded by rough streets and harsh realities: stories of bruises from gang beatings, long hospital recoveries under the pall of the Great Depression, and the grim imprints of war in post-conflict Europe. Even then, his resilience was palpable.

A chance encounter at a boys' club—where a kind woman showed him the magic of reading English—became the first step on a journey that led him from forgotten alleys to the polished halls of the Detroit Athletic Club. His mother, Mary, a determined union organizer who once carried a gun for self-protection, instilled in him a fire for self-discipline and survival. The stiff, divided classrooms at St. Hedwig's— where he was forced to sit behind a glass partition for his father's unbelief—did little to dampen his spirit. Instead, every slight became another brick in the foundation of his determined character.

Richard transformed his early hardships into fuel for growth. He tackled every obstacle with quiet intelligence, dissecting challenges with a researcher's precision while never losing sight of the people whose lives he touched—even if his blunt honesty sometimes cut deeper than he intended.

For years, I made an annual pilgrimage to his farm in Big Rapids. Those visits were filled with long days under the sun, the scent of fresh hay blending with the summer bloom of the flowered arbor, and evenings spent on the porch sharing wine and ideas. We'd debate politics, unravel art, and travel dreams, and reminisce over the loyal companionship of his two beautiful dogs. In those moments, the farm wasn't just land—it was a sanctuary where his steady, unorthodox way of facing life nurtured a bond between us that still comforts me when I face my own crossroads.

I remember one crisp autumn afternoon in the late'90s. As soon as I arrived at the farm to see Richard and Ingrid, he clapped me on the back and said, "Let's go see my son Jerry's new home near Cadillac." With barely a pause, we piled into his old car, the rumble of the engine and the eager barks of his dogs setting the tone for an unexpected adventure. Instead of turning right as planned, Richard steered left toward a local store. He emerged with bottles of beer and whiskey tucked under his arm, and soon enough, we found ourselves at John's trailer—a cozy outpost on the edge of a state reserve where the scent of venison stew mingled with the sharp autumn air.

As the afternoon folded into night, laughter, clinking bottles, and shared stories filled the space until we realized how late it had grown. When we eventually returned to the farm, a worried Ingrid met us at the door. "Where have you been?" she demanded, eyes wide. Thinking fast, we spun a half-joking tale about losing the dogs deep in the reserve. The tension eased, and later that evening we gathered around a full dinner prepared by Ingrid, our earlier misadventure already transforming into the stuff of family legend.

Richard was more than just a mentor—he was my guide through life's unpredictable turns and a partner in moments of reckless celebration. His passion sometimes spilled over: whether he was teaching at the university, prospecting for uranium, or simply sharing drinks on a cool night, he lived as though every moment was both a lesson and a victory. His flaws—the excesses, the moments of indifference—were as integral to him as his hard-won wisdom.

Years later, returning from a trip to Canada during hunting season, I found myself at another lively gathering. Richard and John were hosting a party at the campsite, where about thirty close friends swayed under a pale moon. The celebrations stretched into the early hours, and while I paid for the night with a pounding head for days, I cherished the reckless freedom of it all. To remember that night, I later sent John a set of longhorn antlers I'd picked up in San Antonio, now mounted on his barn—an ever-present memento of shared mischief.

Richard altered my values and goals in the most unanticipated ways. In the gentle rustle of Big Rapids' trees, in the taste of a well-shared bottle of wine, and in every story told under an open sky, his spirit lives on—a reminder that resilience, with a touch of wildness can color even the darkest corners of life.

BOBBY— THE SNAPSHOT

Aunt Clara sat at the kitchen table, carefully sorting through decades of family photographs. The crisp pages, softened by time, were neatly piled for grandchildren and kin. As the last surviving sibling from a family that had journeyed from Europe, every picture carried a quiet weight of remembrance. Amid the faded portraits, a tiny, worn snapshot caught her eye—a picture of Little Bobby, his striped trousers showing a small tear. In that moment, she recalled Sylvia's gentle hands smoothing his hair with Vaseline, the sound of her laughter echoing from years past. Aunt Clara gave the pictures to Rosemary to pass them on.

Rosemary took the pictures home and sifted through them. When she picked up the snapshot of Little Bobby, a flood of memories returned. She recalled the time he had put gum in her hair when the family went to the movies—she was the one who got in trouble, not Bobby. Sibling rivalry, of course. There were happy memories too: taking him to Senate Coney Island for a hot dog or to the Senate Sweet Shop for a banana split sundae; as children sitting together at the dining room table, working on puzzles while listening to "Let's Pretend" on the radio.

She also remembered her time as an usher at the Riviera Theatre, sneaking him in for free and giving him a few nickels for candy. When he was four, she had once tricked him into sticking his finger into an empty lamp socket—with the power still on. He had always been too trusting, easily talked into taking risks. Later, when he was a little older, he turned the tables on her by threatening to tell their mother that she had been necking with boys in the theater—unless she gave him money for candy. He had learned that trick from their older brother, Wally.

Enough reminiscing. Rosemary gathered all the pictures related to Bobby, placed them in a plain brown envelope, and mailed them off to him in Texas—far from where all these memories had been made.

When I returned from a long business trip, a plain brown envelope from Rosemary was on my desk. I never expected anything from her apart from the usual birthday card with a few scratch-off lottery tickets. Curious, I opened the envelope. The smell of old paper and ink immediately pulled me back. My fingers lingered on the familiar snapshot of Little Bobby. I remembered the day it was taken at Woolworth's on Grand River Avenue, the cramped space as I dared a smile for a split second of immortality.

I enlarged the tiny photo and set it in a frame on my bookshelf. Every time a sunbeam lit its tiny face, I could almost hear the distant echoes of childhood—of mischief shared over stolen candy, of challenges during long summer afternoons, and of the raw, unvarnished promise of youth. In that quiet moment, I realized that the boy in the photo was not just a memory, but a reminder of the roads taken, the mistakes made, and the adventures yet to come.

LINDA— A BIOGRAPHY

April 4, 2003

Linda lit up every room she entered—from her restless childhood on the road to the comforting rhythm of family life. Born into constant movement, her early years blurred into a succession of schools and new beginnings. By four, she devoured books as if each page held a secret meant only for her, a quiet promise of the future.

In 1952, when her family finally settled in Lafitte, Louisiana, her father launched a construction business that anchored them for decades. Though money was always tight, Linda's sharp mind and fierce curiosity shone through. In high school she edited the school paper with an intensity that hinted at her dream of studying journalism in the East—a dream eventually rerouted by life. Instead, she enrolled at a junior college briefly before returning to New Orleans, first as a secretary at her father's firm and later at Boeing's Michoud Facility. Wherever she went, Linda nurtured friendships as vividly as she curated memories.

Recalling her first real love—the gentle excitement in her eyes when she met Bob, a fresh-faced electrical engineer straight from military service and graduation. By 1964, they were married, and soon after, Huntsville became their first home. Through the tender chaos of raising Andrea and later Daniel, the scent of barbecue on lazy summer evenings and the clink of glasses at neighborhood cookouts, they built a life that balanced ambition with warmth.

When they moved to Greenhills, Ohio, Linda embraced community with vigor. She wrote columns for the local journal, organized PTA events, and even dabbled in a city council race—losing by a hair's breadth. Yet every setback only spurred her on. In 1974, back in New Orleans, when uncertainty hung thick in the air, Bob's prodding, nudged her into a new chapter at Holy Cross College. In a burst of determination, she finished her degree in three years, soon finding her calling at Belle Chasse Middle School. Later, after long nights at the University of New Orleans, she earned her master's in gifted education—with honors, of course. For over twenty years, she shaped lives with the quiet power of a dedicated teacher.

THE PAPERS

It was 7:45 p.m. on April 3, 2003, the hour when Linda slipped quietly away. I sat in her room, the air heavy with unspoken farewells, as family gathered, and the hospice nurse moved methodically through the routine of paperwork. I handed over Linda's willed-body documents, clumsily bundled with a paper clip. But as soon as the nurse finished, I discovered they were missing.

Within minutes, the room transformed into a flurry of questions and hurried searches—Andrea and her husband Jesse, her brother Bill, even the nurse herself. We scoured every nook: behind the bed's imposing headboard, under piled papers on her desk, inside the nurse's briefcase. It was as if the documents had vanished into thin air.

The next day when Daniel moved in, he eyed the space beneath the bed and said, "Dad, look." There they were—a neat stack of papers, perfectly aligned with the baseboard, as though placed there deliberately. I murmured, "Finally found them," but Daniel's tone was cautious. "There's no way they slipped under like that…" he said, almost questioning the laws of possibility.

I'd always prided myself on order, even if Linda often chided me for discarding her papers and magazines too soon. Now, faced with this unexplained return of her words from the night she passed, I felt a strange pull—a soft, almost imperceptible suggestion that perhaps her love still lingered, reaching out beyond the boundaries of life and death. I had been an agnostic, dismissing the notion of souls and miracles. Yet that moment made me pause. Had Linda left a final message?

JIM AND LORRIE

Our lives, intertwined with friends who had become family, carried echoes of our earlier adventures. Linda and I clashed in our early marriage, but we soon found kindred spirits in Jim and Lorrie. I remember our first California trip vividly—a summer drive up to Yosemite from Pasadena. Earlier, Linda and I shared dinner with Jim and Lorrie, the gentle hum of conversation punctuated by spontaneous laughter.

"Come on, Linda—don't let the road tame you," Lorrie would tease as we wound along the river road, the scent of pine and wet earth filling the air. Yet, when night fell at a ramshackle cabin in Yosemite, the adventure turned raucous. Jim's snoring rattled the walls; Lorrie's half-asleep shouts, "Jim! Jim! Jim!" sparked a late-night scramble as I fumbled outside, eventually sleeping in the car under a starry sky.

We returned to Pasadena with stories that had grown with every retelling—like the time we sped along the river, our laughter mingling with the rush of wind, promising to share our honest thoughts on every misadventure. Trips to Yellowstone and Plymouth, lazy weekends in

Vegas filled with craps and three-card poker—those memories are dear and enduring.

Linda's life was a tapestry woven from small, vivid moments—the vibrant clamor of family life, quiet acts of rebellion and tenderness, and those rare instances when the ordinary lifted into something transcendent. As I look through her pictures, favorite notes and papers on the shelf, I wonder if perhaps, in even the smallest twist of fate, there lies a reminder that love outlives us all.

In every step, Linda taught us to seek beauty in the unexpected, to hold memories close even as we moved on, and to cherish the warmth that lingers long after the final goodbye.

DELINDA— INTERNET, NOT DELETED

Two weeks after Linda passed, I set out to retrace our footsteps—New Orleans, Huntsville, Cincinnati, Longview, and finally back to Houston. Every mile was steeped in memories and quiet tears, an inescapable tribute to her absence.

By summer, with Daniel having moved out, a new presence arrived at home: Suki, a sixteen-year-old exchange student from Hong Kong. I still remember our first weekend together at the Alabama Bookstore in Montrose. His eyes widened at every design book I picked up for him, and in that shared silence, he quickly became the son I never had. A welcome contrast to Daniel and our constant battles.

That fall, longing for another kindred spirit, I ventured online seeking a companion. By Thanksgiving, Suki and I planned a Christmas trip to California. I had meticulously deleted all my online ties with women before the trip. On our return, one profile had stubbornly refused to vanish, it was DeLinda.

In January, we met for coffee at the Barnes& Noble just across from the Galleria. She was in her early sixties, elegantly dressed with a smile that warmed the chill of winter. Over steaming cups, she recounted years spent in AA—twenty-six of them—as well as her battles with lung and breast cancer, hip replacements, and the early demons of alcohol abuse. Once a scholarship student at Rice, a talented musician in the Houston Youth Orchestra, life had tossed her curveballs: unexpected pregnancies, multiple marriages, and a rocky stint in a law firm before she rediscovered her strength through sobriety.

Before long, DeLinda became not only my confidante but a true friend. Over the next four years, our lives intermingled—trips to Europe, long evenings playing bridge, and alternating seasons between Michigan's brisk charm and Texas's gentle warmth. Together, we even penned plays; one found life on a local stage in Montrose.

After only a few weeks of visits, she moved in with me in The Woodlands. My daughter's protest rang out, "You didn't even ask my permission for her to move in!" I fired back, half-joking, "I don't need anyone's permission to do what feels right." In our unconventional little family, marriage had never been the goal anyway.

Evenings often found us listening to the soft notes of her piano as we savored late-night trips to casinos, shared adventurous meals, and celebrated Christmas with family and laughter. Then one summer, during a chill boat cruise at Pictured Rocks in Michigan, a sudden heaviness took hold. That night at the hotel, DeLinda's breath became shallow. A rushed trip to MD Anderson later confirmed what we feared—the lung cancer had returned. In the following months, her strength waned, yet we clung to moments of unexpected humor and tenderness.

One afternoon, as she settled into her old recliner, I leaned over and said, "When you meet God, tell him that if he'd given you better data, you'd have made better choices." She gave me a long, reflective look before asking, "Where'd you hear that?" I grinned and replied, "If it works, I'll use it." Her laughter, soft and knowing, was a small comfort in those bittersweet moments.

DeLinda slipped away just before Thanksgiving. Even now, I sometimes wonder how different her story might have been if we had met as bright-eyed teenagers—she was stunning back then.

Note: Suki finished eleventh grade in The Woodlands, I arranged for him to complete high school in Vancouver and later studied architecture at Cardiff University. Today, he works as an architect in Tokyo, married and has become active in Hong Kong's anti–China takeover movement. He made their list—and my admiration as a human being.

MOVING ON— FALL 2008

DeLinda had passed away last November—just before Thanksgiving— and as I packed up memories in that silent apartment, I found myself strangely eager to leave the past behind. I planned to stay until my lease ended in early May, even as my daughter Andrea's empty house beckoned.

Miguel coaxed me back to Axiom Technologies, Inc. on a part-time basis—helping with minor reorganizations and product design—while he and Nicole navigated the storm of his upcoming divorce. I even reactivated my P. E. license, squeezing in hours of continuing education to meet renewal deadlines. Work, though steady, couldn't quite quiet the echoes of loss.

Leslie, a longtime friend of DeLinda, kept dropping by. We found brief solace at midnight Mass on Christmas Eve and laughed our way through a New Year's Eve comedy show. I even tutored her sons, Adam and Evan, relishing those small moments of normalcy. Yet by March, over a quiet dinner where the conversation hesitated around unspoken disappointments, I realized our connection had run its course. We parted amicably—two souls still mourning DeLinda's absence.

Desperate for something new, I ventured back into dating. Pamela, from West Galveston Island, soon occupied a promising corner of my life. Her family lived just a stone's throw from my new Houston apartment on Westheimer near Beltway 8, and our early encounters felt full of possibility. On April 1, I began a full-time contract at EDG Consultant Engineers. Though I struggled a bit with the cadence of a structured schedule, life's pieces were slowly clicking into place.

But with Pamela, uncertainty hovered. Her birthday on June 1 passed with a pleasant meal and soft laughter, yet my own birthday sank in with quiet disappointment—she forgot to reach out until days later. I tried voicing my concerns: the distance between Galveston and

Houston, her perpetual preoccupation, the silent hint that her heart might belong elsewhere. Her replies were gentle dismissals, lost in the hum of everyday obligations.

One weekend, when Pamela cancelled our plans for her mother's wedding anniversary, I found myself alone. With no destination in mind, I drove to The Woodlands. I sat on a weathered bench near the spot where I had scattered Linda's and Mr. Chips' ashes, letting the autumn wind carry my conversations with God if he was listening! In that solitude, the path ahead began to clear.

Earlier that day, I'd visited TNT for a quick nail appointment—and that's when I reconnected with Linh. I gave her an old CD by mistake, and later, as I drove along I-45, my phone rang. Linh's soft voice asked why I'd returned her gift. The misunderstanding soon melted away over an invitation to dinner at Red Lobster on FM1960. The next evening, our conversation spilled effortlessly over coffee at Starbucks. Linh, in halting English and warm laughter, unfolded stories of her past relationships and the hardships she'd weathered. There were moments when her voice quivered, only to be shrugged off with a wry, "Just a woman thing."

Wednesday night, as Linh prepared to leave for Saigon for her daughter's wedding—with a promise to be back by July 12—she asked if I was still tangled up with Pamela. I admitted I was, and her reply was gentle yet insistent: if I wanted something real, I should end that chapter.

That Friday, Pamela invited me over for the weekend—a hopeful prelude to intimacy. I delayed, claiming a few loose ends I needed to fix. We had a pleasant afternoon: a steak dinner, a movie we'd both anticipated. But as night fell, I broke the news softly that we should take a break until the fall. The moment froze, her eyes flickering with unspoken hurt as she busied herself with an issue on her speaker system. The next morning, I left a note and slipped out before she awoke.

Exchanged emails later carried the heavy whisper of unfulfilled expectations. In one message, I recalled the opera we'd attended—the night fate seemed intent on laying obstacles in our path. I confessed a deep void, a yearning to simply feel numb. Though she read my words as anger, I was only disappointed that love couldn't conquer the inevitable. In my final email to her, I wrote that I'd always think of her fondly, but it was time to move on. The following day, Pamela's digital presence was erased—gone with a few clicks.

That evening, a call from my brother Gerry shifted my perspective. He reminded me of Linh, who was due back next month from Saigon. The thought stirred a quiet hope.

Over the years I'd spent in Houston—juggling work and personal dilemmas—I'd often met Carolyn Wynn for advice. One session, as we dissected the tangled mess of my relationships, she looked me square in the eye and said, "You need to get away from Pamela as fast as you can!" That truth led me to cleanse my online contacts, even as Carolyn warned me about the 26-year age difference between Linh and me. In that moment, my heart had other, immediate priorities.

FAMILY MATTERS

Meanwhile, Linh had been caring for her mother, Do, next door on Ella Boulevard in Spring, Texas. With her sisters Vy and My in Foley, Alabama, Linh saw a chance for a fresh start—and perhaps a new business venture. We completed the maze of paperwork to transfer Do's housing and support services from Texas to Alabama. In Houston, her sister Tammy remained indifferent, and Do's boyfriend, Matthew, only complicated matters further.

I rented a truck and helped pack Do's belongings. With Linh's brother Thuan's efficient hand and her sister My's husband Roger taking turns at the wheel, we drove the truck to Foley. There, sister Vy took charge, moving Do into an apartment and discarding what wasn't needed—a decision I came to respect.

Linh and I on an earlier visit bought a home on County Road 12—a hidden gem amid a collapsing housing market in 2009. My son Daniel visited frequently from New Orleans; his unruly ways and ongoing money troubles eventually grew too disruptive. As business prospects with Linh's sisters fell through, she returned to the nail salons in Foley, weighed down by disappointments. After seven years, craving change, we sold the house and set our sights on California, where her daughter Quynh awaited. By December 2015, we were on the road in Linh's Honda Element, towing a small trailer. I later cleared out Foley with one final truckload of memories, and in that move, my turbulent relationship with Daniel quietly ended.

Foley had once been the backdrop for family dinners, birthdays, and visits from relatives spanning Houston to Vietnam. I still remember commuting twice a month to Houston, working remotely for EDG Engineering and Axiom Technologies—a generally happy period, punctuated by the steady pulse of family life.

Each mile, each encounter, carried its own bittersweet melody—a farewell to the old and a tentative greeting to what lay ahead. And in that uncertain dance between loss and new beginnings, I learned that sometimes, moving on means embracing every unexpected turn with both caution and hope.

HONDA ELEMENT

In-December 2015, we hit the road for California in Linh's Honda Element, towing a trailer crammed with her life. Our move wasn't the end of everything—just the latest chapter. Back in Foley, a careless joke had sparked a rift. One day at the kitchen table, Linh mentioned buying Quynh's Mini Cooper and proposed that I take the Element in exchange for $12,000. I cracked, "Wait a minute—I already paid $15,000 for it!" My words, meant in jest, struck a wrong chord. Linh's eyes flashed, and she threatened to leave with nothing but her backpack. I called on her sister Vy to smooth things over, but the damage was done. The fallout was a chilly two-day drive to California—a silence that echoed her unresolved hurt.

Back in 2009, when our life together was still new, I'd swept away debts—a car loan and a sum owed to her mother—so that we could begin fresh in Foley, Alabama, close to her sisters. But years in Foley had eroded Linh's hope, until the pull of Quynh in California became irresistible. Amid our heated exchange, I remembered how limited her

English made misunderstandings more acute, and how a string of failed marriages and painful betrayals had left her wary. I had once believed I could show her that not all men were selfish or controlling. Somehow, we were still finding our footing.

After retrieving our scattered belongings and settling at Quynh's, a tentative truce emerged. We agreed that once I returned with everything, we'd live upstairs for six months to let the tempers cool and the past recede.

THE DELUGE

Our new California life took a chaotic turn one ordinary Thursday. Our townhome in Riverside—a modest two-level, three-bedroom gem we'd renovated after a 2016 trip to Italy—hummed with routine. My granddaughter Chloe, now seven and full of restless energy, discovered a tiny stain on the bathroom ceiling and shouted, "Bobby, look at that spot!" The mark was no larger than a dime—a leak from the upstairs bathroom. With Linh's son Khanh and his friend Vinh set to depart Monday morning, I scheduled a plumber for an inspection.

Late Monday morning, the plumber, tool belt jingling, followed me to the bathroom. Within minutes, he pulled down a section of ceiling board—and out spilled a writhing swarm of termites. I remember my heart stopped as I stood frozen, staring at the chaos unfolding.

As the plumber searched for the leak's source, Linh's voice cut through the tension. "I've got friends coming for lunch at noon," she told me. I insisted, "We need to move that gathering—this isn't the place right now." Her frustration escalated into loud and heated words that filled the narrow space. The plumber, distracted, accidentally nicked a fire suppression line. Suddenly, water burst from the ceiling, cascading across the dining room floor in a surging torrent.

In a flurry of urgency, he darted outside to shut off the main water supply. But before he could repair the cut line, someone in another unit turned the valve back on. The resulting pressure—an unforgiving water hammer—burst the pipe. Within moments, water was flooding the entire dining room and spilling out the front door. At that exact instant, Linh's guests arrived, stepping into a deluge of water. The plumber, now flustered, raced back as the fire department's lights began to flash outside.

Eventually, Linh gathered her guests and left with Khanh and Vinh, leaving me to oversee the carnage. The plumber fixed the suppression line and traced the leak back to a poorly installed drain line—an error from the original builder six years earlier. Though he later handed me a $7,000 cash settlement, I knew deep down that blaming him alone wouldn't set things right. Had Linh's anger not turned our conversation into a shouting match, the plumber might have focused solely on the leak.

That afternoon, I hired a seasoned contractor to dry out walls, remediate mold, and repair the damaged ceiling, flooring, and drywall—a two-week ordeal costing nearly $12,000. I kept the townhome until summer before eventually selling it and returning to Alabama in January.

Looking back, I can't help but wonder: If Chloe had not noticed that tiny stain, if I'd scheduled the plumber a day later, or if Linh had simply agreed to postpone lunch without a fight—perhaps none of this would have happened. In the end, poor planning, heated distractions, and an inflexible state of mind, set off a chain reaction neither of us could have predicted.

ANDREA

Andrea's high school days flowed by in a mix of Girl Scout meetings, school clubs, and quiet afternoons that hinted at the determination inside her. Later, at Baylor in Waco, she pursued speech pathology with a focus that belied the turbulence of her early adulthood. I'd warned her before her first marriage—a union I doubted even then—that she needed time to discover who she truly was. Eight years later, after her husband in Atlanta had drained her bank accounts and shattered their shared dreams, I remember her sitting in the den and whispering, "I told you so."

Despite the haze of our New Orleans years—years marked by my own frequent absences—Andrea found her footing. Even though I once wished she'd headed to Clemson instead of Louisiana Tech, where she met Phil, she reclaimed control over her life with a strength that slowly transformed her pain into purpose.

DANIEL

Daniel's life, in stark contrast, became a storm of late nights and reckless abandon after our move to New Orleans. Parties and cheap alcohol blurred the edges of responsibility, and arguments with Andrea became a regular soundtrack at home. When he announced his wish to attend Loyola, I could not hold back: "Absolutely not! You're meant to leave— to see something different!" I forced him to consider colleges far from the chaos—Colby in New England, Georgia, Alabama—anything to save our fragile peace.

He eventually earned a degree in political science, flirted with a legal career, then settled into teaching high school. Yet old habits persisted like a stubborn shadow. By 2015, the mounting turbulence forced me into an agonizing decision: love sometimes means stepping away when the hurt grows too deep.

PIDDY

In the midst of these human storms, a small black-and-white kitten named Piddy came into our lives—an unexpected beacon of gentle mischief. My son's secret rescue of a stray, hidden from a crowded garage sale, blossomed into a twenty-year companionship neither Linda or I anticipated.

Piddy had a quiet way of weaving into everyday moments. He'd nestle in the clean laundry basket, curl up under the utility sink, or engage in playful skirmishes with Frisky or Mr. Chips, our perfect dogs.

I still chuckle remembering the night Bandit—a scrappy cat from across the street—sent Susan our neighbor, racing over in alarm, thinking she had run over Piddy, it was bandit. Piddy was unscathed under the sink. If it was the other way, Linda would have killed me.

Even when he vanished from our Trophy Club condo, sending me crisscrossing neighborhood streets in a fruitless search, his eventual return felt like a small miracle—a reminder that even in a chaotic world, there's solace to be found in unexpected places.

In each life—Andrea's rediscovery of herself, Daniel's tumultuous quest for direction, and Piddy's quiet, resilient presence, we witness the delicate interplay of loss and hope. Their stories, so different yet intertwined by the passage of time, remind me that moving forward often means embracing both our mistakes and our moments of unexpected grace.

1944: Rosemary at 11

Mid- 1990s: Rosemary, Wally– Bob & Gerry

Early 2000s: Richard & John– Richard

The Farm near Big Rapids– Bob, Ingrid & Rosemary

Linda 1994

2005 Bob & DeLinda

2011 Linh New Orleans

2023 Linh

Mr. Chips & Piddy

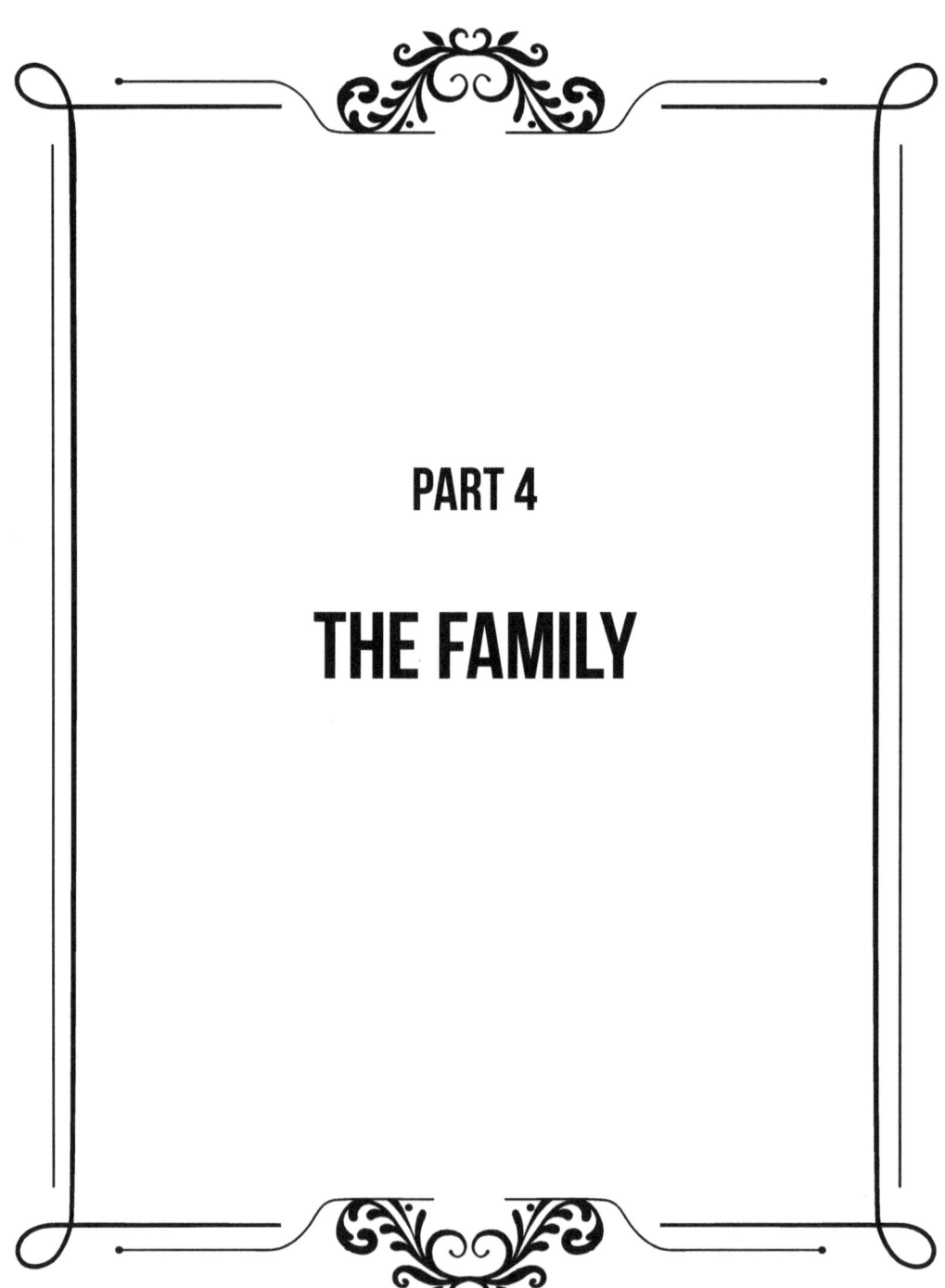

PART 4

THE FAMILY

A GIFT FROM KATHERINE

In the soft glow of afternoon light, I stared at an old cross—dark wood, about eighteen inches tall, adorned with sixteen mother-of-pearl buttons and crowned by a small cast figure of Christ. It rested silently on a rectangular base atop the chest of drawers, a relic that carried more than just memories—it carried a lifetime of quiet prayers.

I picked it up and recalled the stories told by my mother and Aunt Clara about Grandma Katherine, who had received this cross in Krakow when she was fifteen in 1894. I could almost hear the gentle rustle of her skirts and the soft murmur of her prayers as she clutched it close, dreaming of a future with Jozef. On long, stormy nights aboard a creaking ship, she had prayed for lost children, later for her ailing husband, and for strength when even her own sons turned against her during the Depression. Each scratch on the wood and each glint of mother-of-pearl spoke of hope, sorrow, and unwavering faith.

Now, in 2006, after surviving generations of grief and fleeting joy, the cross awaited its next chapter. It had been passed, with careful hands and tender words, from Aunt Clara to Rosemary—and now it was destined for great-great-granddaughter Katy. I sat there, tracing its worn edges, and wondered if someday Katy would feel the same quiet reassurance that once buoyed Katherine through the darkest of nights.

YOUNG SYLVIA

It was a warm summer in 1926 Detroit when Sylvia, barely sixteen, moved through her days with a quiet determination. At dawn, while most teenagers slept in, she was already washing clothes by hand, scrubbing dishes, and helping her mother keep the house in order. The sound of splashing soapy water and the steady thrum of the city formed the soundtrack of her early life—a life burdened yet filled with small, secret hopes.

Born into a crowded home where her mother, Katherine, bore twenty-three children, Sylvia learned early that survival meant sacrifice.

In a family where grief was as common as laughter—seven children lost in infancy, others fading too soon—each day was both a struggle and a quiet act of bravery. She found a small refuge in routine: a worn handkerchief tucked in her pocket, a secret smile shared over a meager slice of bread, a brief moment by the window watching the world beyond.

Then came Walter. Their wedding night turned bitter when, in the stark morning light, he called her "damaged goods" over a broken hymen—a single, cruel remark that shattered any promise of tenderness. In the hush that followed, her father Josef's pleading words blended with the distant toll of a church bell. Although a kindly priest later suggested other possibilities, the damage was irrevocable. Sylvia's future, once bright with youthful possibility, now carried a heavy, silent ache.

As the Great Depression crept in and the world around her darkened—with the crash of the stock market and the relentless hardships that followed—Sylvia learned to bury her disappointment beneath endless chores. Yet in the quiet moments, when a soft breeze stirred the worn pages of an old prayer book, she'd close her eyes and imagine a different life—one where kindness and hope could still bloom amidst sorrow.

In these intertwined lives—the enduring legacy of Katherine's cross and the tender resilience of young Sylvia—we glimpse a family forged by both strength and heartache. Their stories, etched into familiar objects and quiet actions, whisper of past struggles and hint at the promise of a future where every sacrifice carries the seed of a new beginning.

WIFE AND MOTHER

I have no idea of how those first harsh years of the Depression were survived—only that by 1933 my father finally landed a job as a milkman at Family Creamery. He worked long, grueling days—delivering milk, juggling accounts, and catching sleep in stolen moments—anything to keep the family afloat. Slowly, with FDR's steady leadership and the looming promise of a world at war, life began to ease its grip on us.

At home, Sylvia—ever the tireless worker—filled our days with the rhythms of domestic life. She scrubbed clothes by hand in the basement, the scent of Fels-Natha mingling with the damp chill of stone; twice a week, she hung laundry on a creaky clothesline, her hands steady despite the bitter cold or relentless sun. Evenings were punctuated by the comforting murmur of the radio: Breakfast in Hollywood gave way to The Breakfast Club, then to quiet stories and gentle prayers. In stolen moments, she'd slip away for a pastry run or share a laugh with neighbor Violet—a brief pause from a life spent shouldering endless responsibility.

Yet beneath the routine lay quiet heartache. Sylvia never learned to drive, always too nervous behind the wheel, and her marriage with Walter was a battleground from the start. Even their wedding night had sown betrayal—a broken hymen and harsh words branded her as "damaged goods." Her father's gentle counsel and a priest's soft explanation couldn't erase the lasting sting. Over the years, as the war ended and modern appliances eased the daily grind, the love and bitter rivalry between Sylvia and Walter remained. One incident—Walter's rough handling of Sylvia causing such a commotion that neighbor Lynn had to call firefighters—marked the last time physical abuse touched their lives. He later managed to buy a modest house on Julian, then his dream home on Coyle Avenue, as children grew into their separate lives, and scandal quietly rocked our family.

When the weight of years and unhealed wounds pressed down, Sylvia's health faltered; chronic pain, arthritis, and Parkinson's eventually tethered her to a wheelchair. Even as Walter briefly wavered on leaving her, he found himself consigned to the role of reluctant caregiver—a role that, despite the bitter echoes of their past, ended with a strange relief when Sylvia's long, torturous battle finally quieted in a nursing home. I still remember her sigh of release, mingled with the silence of a love that had always been as much about pain as it was about survival.

THE FIRST ENCOUNTER

It was early November 1942, and I was just five-year-old, traveling with my parents in our 1935 Ford, heading for the hospital across from Grand Circus Park. The rain hammered the windshield as streetlights and traffic lights blurred into a watery mosaic. My father's voice cut through the sound of the wipers, "Stay here and lock the door," as we parked outside the small, three-story hospital—a place that seemed as fragile and uncertain as the hope we clung to that day.

Alone, inside the car, I watched shadows dance on rain-soaked streets until my father returned and broke the silence: my grandmother had died. "I will be back." he said. I remember the rain stopped as my eyes tired with sleep. Then, the abrupt sound of the car door—that moment my mother, overcome with grief, collapsed into the seat, silent tears carving trails down her face.

The journey home was muted except for her tears and lone sorrow. The next evening, we drove to Aunt Clara's modest home in the old Polish quarter, where the only comfort was the flickering warmth of a coal stove in a sparse living area. During the night, I was drawn to the soft glow of candles that framed my grandmother's casket in the front parlor—her pale face bathed in a strange, red-tinted light through glass lenses. I couldn't recall much about her, and the air was heavy with the scent of flowers.

In the hurried moments of the funeral that morning—coffee brewing, pans clattering, the church bell tolling like a slow heartbeat, I watched my family adrift in grief. My father comments on the service and memories from earlier funerals, and my mother, intermittently crying until at the grave site, she fainted against the descending casket, all blended into a single, timeless ache.

Years later, when loss struck again—my wife's passing after a long illness—I found that the tears came unbidden, unstoppable. It was only then I began to understand the full weight of grief that had hovered, unrecognized, all those years ago. In the quiet, reflective hours that followed each farewell, I saw clearly the mistakes of my own youth:

the moments I dismissed my mother's love, the stubborn distance I maintained against the tide of familial pain. I now carry those memories gently, a reminder of how even in our darkest moments, we are bound together by love and loss.

ENVIRONMENT

I remember piecing together the fragments of our past—stories passed down in hushed tones and bitter recollections of a harsh home life. My father's earliest memories were shrouded in cold winters and even colder hearts. When Walter was just fourteen in January 1918, his mother, Antonina, was dying of tuberculosis. I can still hear his trembling confession to his father, Joseph: "I wish it were you instead of her." In the years that followed, his sisters—Bernice, Helen, and Victoria—succumbed to TB and infection, leaving Walter with a simmering resentment. He later blamed Joseph for keeping the house frigid, for forcing his married sister to use her own dishes in an unforgiving, thrift-ridden household.

Yet even amidst that bitterness, there were rare warm memories. In Chicago, my father's Aunt Mary and her daughters—Wanda and Cassie—crafted a home steeped in Polish traditions but glowing with genuine care. I recall sitting on the worn sofa at their place, wide-eyed as Wanda regaled me with stories of a kinder world.

Walter's own childhood was a battleground. As the oldest of seven, he was forced by his strict, battered father to surrender every penny he earned at the CM Hall Lamp Company until, at eighteen, when he dared ask to keep some wages—Joseph's reply was to send him away. I remember the sting of those words echoed in family tales, and the way discipline was meted out with a leather cat-o'-nine-tails kept hidden in a locked cabinet until rebellious hands shattered it into pieces, only for the belt to reappear when needed.

At our home on Julian, the ritual was unchanging: recalling how Walter would lash out with his belt on my brothers and even Rosemary—who once, for daring to wear jeans, was dragged home by her hair. I can still picture the cold silence that followed, the weight of his words— "This is the dumbest of my children"—a phrase that would haunt Rosemary for years. Despite it all, she survived, building a tough shell to guard her tender heart. I think she was damaged most from that early environment.

I recall one stormy Texas day on a trip from Fredericksburg to Houston, with Rosemary, Stuart, DeLinda, and me. We had planned for an overnight stay in San Antonio. A forecast of heavy rain had us scrambling at the Riverwalk Mall for shelter, only to be caught in an unyielding downpour. Drenched and desperate, we eventually sought refuge at a McDonald's—where Rosemary, her pride as wet as the night, ended up arguing with the manager over the temperature of a cup of coffee. Such moments, chaotic and poignant, defined the ragged edges of our lives.

For me, Little Bobby—the world with Walter was different. He and I shared moments listening to Tiger baseball on the radio, the simple joy of fishing on the St. Clair River, and even the steady routine of his milk route in Hamtramck. From ages seven to seventeen, I worked as his jumper, absorbing lessons through conversations, his gentle corrections, and even his rare smiles. He never raised his voice with me the way he did with my siblings. I remember one call—a rare slip between us— when, exasperated, I muttered, "God damn it, Dad, that's not true!" and he chastised me for using bad language. I regretted that slip, a small crack in what was otherwise a tender bond.

Walter carried deep wounds. He resented our distance—me chasing a career and life's dreams in New Orleans and Houston, Rosemary anchored at home, and Wally and Gerry scattered by ambition and rebellion. It wasn't about money; it was a bitter sense of abandonment. His solitary meals at greasy McDonald's contrasted sharply with our days at steakhouses, a constant reminder that we had forgotten to care for him. Yet, in quieter moments, I saw that beneath the tough exterior was a man who had loved fiercely—a man who had once taken me to Detroit Tigers games, went bowling with me, and fished side by side, sharing stories of a life he'd once dreamed could be different.

A FINAL NOTE ABOUT WALTER

Looking back through old photographs of my father and me, I now understand how deeply he cared. Our moments together—carousel rides, quiet night fishing on the St. Clair River, the steadfast presence on his milk route—shaped my character. He taught me resilience, the value of hard work, and the silent power of a shared smile. Even though his relationship with my siblings was marred by cruelty and discipline, he reserved a different kind of love for me. I remember the gentle way he guided me through life's lessons, the subtle nod when I succeeded, and even the quiet rebuke when I strayed.

Even as I grew older and our paths diverged, I held onto those memories. In the silence of my recollections, I realized that our family's past—filled with harsh words, broken promises, and deep wounds—had also given us moments of unexpected tenderness. And though the ghosts of those years still linger, they have taught me that love can exist even in the midst of pain, and that forgiveness is a small light in a dark room.

Now, when I hear echoes of my father's voice in a distant crowd, or see a well-worn belt in a dusty cabinet, I know that the past has not been erased. It lives on in the silent spaces between our words and in the gentle, even if imperfect, gestures that continue to bind us together.

In the end, my family's story is a mosaic of hardship and resilience—a place where cold discipline met small acts of love, and where even the darkest memories held a glimmer of hope for redemption.

JOSEPH FURMAGA—A SHORT BIOGRAPHY AND NOTES

My earliest memory of my grandfather dates back to 1940 when I was about four years old. I recall stepping over a faded rug in his modest Detroit home on Junction, near Michigan Avenue. The house was simple—bead curtains swaying in doorways, a large, imposing black safe in the dining room, and an old nutcracker dog. I remember once pinching my fingers while playing with that dog and crying until my father came to my rescue—a small, vivid moment that still connects me to those early days.

Grandpa Joseph never spoke English but flowed comfortably between Polish and Russian. I remember visiting him, watching him sit at the worn wooden kitchen table as he read a newspaper, or savoring his simple breakfast of black bread, hard salami, and a steaming cup of coffee. Every Sunday, my mother Sylvia would always set aside a warm plate for his noontime meal. I still remember riding in our 1935 Ford—and later in Walter's 1948 Pontiac—carefully holding that plate on my lap as we drove the three miles to his house. When I stepped inside and softly said "hello," he'd grant me a small smile, a quiet acknowledgment of our bond.

As I grew older, questions about his origins began to surface. My father Walter shared little, leaving the tapestry of his past to be woven from family stories. When my sister Rosemary started dating Richard Dudek in late 1949, our family learned, much to our surprise, that Richard's mother—Mary Dudek, living behind St. Hedwig's Church on Wesson Avenue—had known Grandpa Joseph. Over the years, Richard would recount evenings spent with him, unraveling tales of his early days in Poland and Russia. Those moments, shared between us over coffee, slowly filled in the gaps of a life I had only glimpsed in old photographs.

Piecing together what little was known, I discovered that Joseph was born around 1876 on a small farm in Poland—a rugged beginning that set the tone for his hard-lived life. Abandoned by his parents when he was just seven, he and his brother Frank were left behind as his parents moved to Warsaw with their daughter. At sixteen, when Russian authorities came calling for military service, fate intervened: the farmer's son was to be conscripted, but Joseph was sent in his place. Joseph served in the Russian army in East Russia, only to later desert and find his way back to Poland. In a small village in the Wielkolas region, he reinvented himself as a police officer and, during the bitter winter of 1902–1903, married Antonina Kloc.

The tide turned in early 1904. With Japan's attack on Port Arthur stirring uncertainty in the Russian ranks, Joseph likely feared forced return to that harsh life. He found his escape in Antwerp, boarding the steamship Finland in early April. After a roughly two-week voyage, his name appeared on the Ellis Island passenger list on April 25, 1904, with his origins marked as Wielkolas and his intended destination as Wheeling, West Virginia—a plan that soon gave way to a new start in Detroit.

In Detroit, Joseph arranged for Antonina and his young son Walter to join him. They sailed the same route, arriving on the Finland on July 5, 1905, and soon, the family began building a new life together. Joseph labored first on the Windsor Tunnel between Detroit and Canada, and later at Ford Motor Company in Highland Park. Wise with his earnings, he invested in rental properties, and by his mid-40s, he managed to retire. He passed away on October 25, 1958, and now rests in Holy Cross Cemetery beside Antonina and their three daughters—a quiet testament to a life of hard work, sacrifice, and survival.

These are the pieces of a puzzle assembled from family memories, conversations with my cousin Wanda in Chicago, and hours spent combing through records on Ancestry.com. Each discovery casts a new light on Joseph's journey—a journey marked by escape, resilience, and the relentless hope of a man who crossed oceans to build something better for his family.

Even now, as I hold onto these stories, I can almost hear his quiet voice, feel the weight of that old safe, and see the gentle rise and fall of his simple, determined life—a legacy that continues to echo through the generations.

ADDITIONAL FINDINGS

While poring over old documents, I uncovered small clues that began to fill in the mosaic of Joseph's life. A World War I draft card from September 1918—registration number 3791—listed his address at 1133 25th Street and confirmed his employment at Ford Motor Company in Highland Park. Scattered passenger lists added unexpected twists: Antonina was recorded traveling alongside Andrew Kalwasinski, and names like Antoni Furmaga and Jan Lukasik appeared, each noting Joseph as a brother or friend. Even Marya Wlykto's travel record linked Joseph as her brother-in-law. These fragments, shared with me by Cousin Wanda and gathered from late-night research sessions, slowly revealed not just facts but the enduring ties of family.

ORIGINS OF THE FURMAGA FAMILY

During a quiet afternoon in Houston, I sat down with Wieslaw Furmaga, who painted a vivid picture of our family's roots in the Bychawa region, just south of Lubin, Poland—a landscape of rolling farmland and stubborn resilience. I learned that, once landowners of a rich but fragile soil, our ancestors lost everything after Napoleon's defeat. When Polish army cadets attempted an uprising on November 29, 1830, it was brutally squashed by May, and suspected rebels were chained and sent to Siberia. Joseph's grandfather was among those who lost his land to Russian officials. In the years that followed, many in our family channeled their lives into a legacy of science, medicine, and music—in WWII they were defiant and worked against Nazi oppression. These words, spoken by Wieslaw, echoed in my mind like a promise that our history, though marred by loss, was equally defined by resilience and hope.

CHESTER (UNCLE CHUCK)

I last saw Uncle Chuck on Julep Lane in Ohio, sometime in the shadowed hours of 1968 or 1969. He'd ring the doorbell, tip his hat with a crooked grin, and vanish before dawn—just another transient visit, a quiet rebellion against routine. His life was a collage of rough edges and laughter. In his early years, he joined the army during the Great Depression, only to later drift into trouble with his drinking; a boozy AWOL, as some would say. He wandered with the circus, riding freight trains, setting up tents under starry skies, even once claiming the identity of a dead man he found in a boxcar. I still remember him laughing through a story about a car accident: "If I hadn't been drunk, I'd be dead," he'd say, his voice a blend of mischief and survival.

Uncle Chuck had a gentle way with his harmonica. I recall a story of when Aunt Clara was just ten, the two of them penned a tune called "Waiting by the Water Tower for a Train," a melody that an early country singer later recorded—a bittersweet echo from days of innocence and wild days on the road. His obituary, printed in the Detroit Free Press on October 21, 1987, captured the essence of his life: a man who volunteered at Detroit Harper Medical Center, handed out gifts to children, and, despite his threadbare clothes, never once denied his kindness.

Each of these discoveries—fact and story alike—adds a layer to the portrait of our family. They remind me that even amid hard times and harsh discipline, there was laughter, rebellion, and an unspoken commitment to endure. And as I piece together these fragments, I sense that the legacy of Joseph, the origins of the Furmaga family, and the irreverent spirit of Uncle Chuck are not just relics of a bygone era but living echoes that will shape our future in unexpected ways.

TIME FOR THE UNEXPLAINED

December 30, 2011

There are moments in life that defy logic, leaving us with puzzles too subtle to understand. I spent quiet hours pondering these mysteries, recalling both my own eerie encounters and the uncanny stories my family has passed down. Among these memories are episodes that still defy an explanation.

A WINTER APPARITION— 1918

My father, Walter—just fourteen then—sitting by the dining room window on a snowy January night in 1918. The snowfall had hushed the world, leaving only the soft glow of a streetlamp. As he skimmed the newspaper, his eyes suddenly fixed on a figure: a man in a dark overcoat, gliding down the street. The stranger paused at the front walk and then advanced along the side of our house. Walter's voice broke the silence as he alerted his father, Joseph, "Someone's at the back." Stepping outside into a world of pristine snow, they discovered a single set of footprints leading up to the back gate—no return tracks, no explanation. In the days that followed, as the house grew silent with loss, Walter's mother, Antonette, passed away from tuberculosis, her final breaths a quiet part of that mysterious winter night.

A DREAM AND A TRAGEDY— 1932

In another reverie from the past, my mother Sylvia once confided a troubling dream. She'd seen a man shot through both wrists—a surreal image that clung to her waking thoughts. That New Year's Eve, as her sister Rose stood alone on her bedroom balcony with her hands clasped tightly, the unexpected sound of a celebratory gunshot shattered the night. A stray bullet went through both of Rose's wrists in a way that mirrored Sylvia's haunting vision. Weeks later, as Rose walked to Sylvia's home under a winter evening sky, a hit-and-run ended her life. Sylvia later named her daughter Rosemary—an echo of hope mingled with sorrow.

A SHATTERED IMAGE— 1940S

In the dim corridors of our family's past, my grandmother Katherine's painful legacy also holds its mysteries. After Joseph Nowacki died in 1934, leaving Katherine to struggle alone during the Depression, with her daughter Clara—then just a teenager—witnessed unspeakable hardships. At one point, a portrait of the Virgin Mary, which had hung faithfully behind Katherine's bed, became a source of curious concern. One heated evening in the late 1940s, after a bitter argument with her husband Frank, Clara discovered the glass protecting the image, shattered and the picture crawling with maggots. She carried it outside and burned it, as if trying to purge a curse from their lives. That same night, a chance reunion with estranged family—sparked by a brief conversation with Silvia and her long-estranged brother Phillip—hinted that even the deepest wounds could begin to heal.

GHOSTS IN THE DIGITAL AGE— 2003

Almost a year had passed since Linda had died and now an enigma that left echoes in unexpected places. Months after her death, I flirted with the idea of returning to Catholicism. I met a confident, independent woman from Brazil online. Weeks passed and one night after coffee, she confided that she sensed Linda's presence lingering in her home and on moonlit walks. "It's like bad karma," she said her eyes clouded with inexplicable worry. Even our movie dates—like the night we watched *Bad Santa*—felt haunted by an unseen force. Months earlier, I asked my sister Rosemary to buy me a crucifix when she was on a trip to Mackinac Bridge, near Holy Cross Village. I discontinued seeing the Brazilian woman. I went to the mailbox one afternoon and there were two boxes waiting. The bottom box contained gifts I had given the Brazilian woman, and the top package contained a stone crucifix, broken at the base—a silent, symbol of lost protection?

A READING OF FATE— 2007

In the autumn of 2007, as DeLinda's lung cancer returned. I found myself drawn to a small house on the I-45 service road near The Woodlands. A faded sign for tarot readings beckoned, and on a chilly November evening I stopped. A young girl, barely eighteen, shuffled me into a corner and began laying out her cards with a soft, unnerving certainty. "Your companion will die before the holidays," she predicted in a hushed tone, her eyes distant yet piercing. A week later, mere days before Thanksgiving, DeLinda passed away. I returned for another reading, only to find the girl gone—replaced by her stepmother, Jennifer, who explained that the readings had lost meaning after the girl's father died. In time, I stopped seeking answers from cards, yet the echo of that prediction—of fate's cold inevitability—remained with me.

In the silent spaces of late nights and dusty records, these events—whether the ghostly footprints in the snow, a prophetic dream turned tragedy, a burned portrait teeming with decay, or warnings whispered over tarot cards—remind me that the unexplained is woven through our lives. Each mystery, each whispered secret from the past, hints at deeper truths about loss, fate, and the enduring pull of memories that refuse to fade. And sometimes, in the interplay between light and shadow, we learn that the unseen holds as much power as the tangible world around us.

Jozef & Katherine

Walter & Sylvia

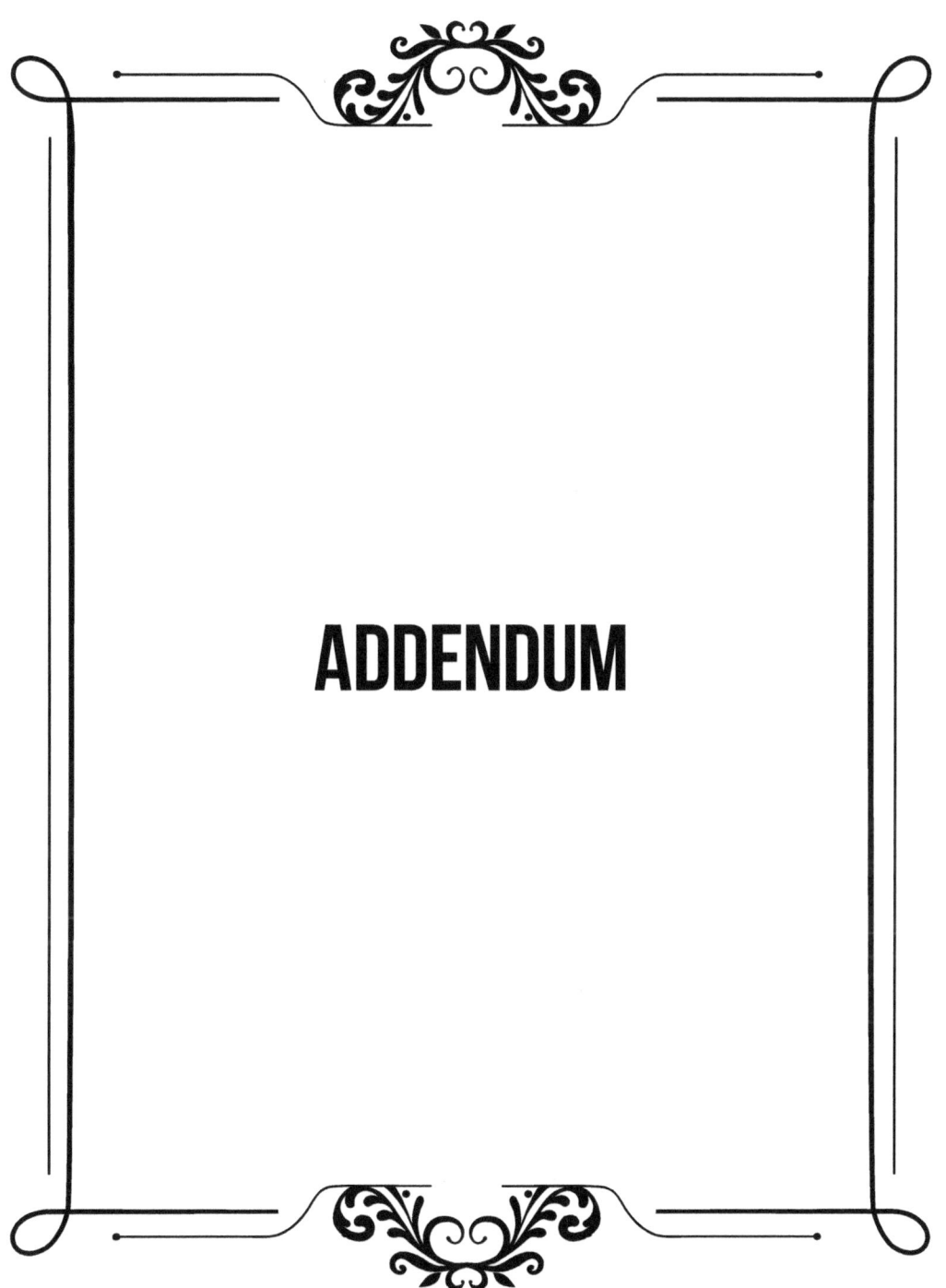

ADDENDUM

AN UPDATE AT EIGHTY SIX

June 9, 2023
My sister Rosemary passed away on May 24 at over ninety years old, following ten long months of a debilitating illness. On my birthday last Monday, I received her final note and $10—an odd reminder that, in our old bet, I'd "won" because she always said she'd go before me. Now, with just a handful of ashes and a flood of memories remaining, I find myself forced to confront loss once again.

In recent years, I've squeezed time back into my studies—diving into particle physics and cosmology, expanding my understanding of an ever-expanding universe destined, in the far future, to decay into nothing. I've always believed life is a one-time gift, measured not by its length but by the impact we have on those we love. Life is as unpredictable as a car accident or a cancer diagnosis; in embracing that, I've learned to live fully in each moment. I recently advised a close friend—just 62, who had survived a stroke—to forget long-term plans and focus on what he could achieve in the coming months.

Now I face another difficult challenge: Linh's cancer. Aging myself, I had never imagined suffering another heartbreak after losing Linda and then DeLinda. Yet as I learn more about Linh's treatments and see the steady progress in her health, I feel a renewed sense of purpose. Linh's inner beauty shines when she smiles or laughs; despite the grim prognosis that she might never become old, her resilience is slowly steering her back to a life of meaningful moments.

THE FINAL CHAPTER

July 15, 2023

At eighty-six, I pause to reflect on the path behind me—a journey carved out of circumstances, some entirely beyond my control. Illness in a spouse, poor decisions by my children, reckless behavior among siblings, and choices by others in business and family have all steered my course. I've learned to set limits on what I can change and to accept the mistakes I made along the way. As a child, I contemplated life and death while discarding the remnants of a painful Catholic upbringing; by sixteen, I was agnostic, and at midlife I drifted in and out of atheism. Through it all, I met remarkable people, embraced education, and discovered that our lives are shaped equally by choice and chance.

I've touched lives—sometimes for better, sometimes with a sting I fully intended. The values my father instilled in me guided my decisions, even as I navigated complex relationships with the three major women in my life: Linda, whose presence was a tumultuous, thirty-eight-year challenge; DeLinda, my steady, kind companion; and Linh, whose wisdom now softens past wounds. I've been disappointed by my siblings' refusal to examine and amend their flaws, even as I tried to maintain boundaries amid the chaos their actions sometimes stirred; remembering my lifelong love for Wally, Gerry and Rosemary was never in doubt.

Linh, for example, has begun to value clear boundaries in her relationship with her daughter Quynh—a change I've witnessed with cautious optimism. We all build our expectations about life and the people in it, yet reality has a way of surprising us. As I now face a future with uncertainties, I am still filled with hope. Of course, I have a few regrets about my past, but as my journey now nears its natural end, I find a quiet relief in knowing I really did try to do my best.

THE VALUE IN THIS JOURNEY

Socrates once declared, "The unexamined life is not worth living." Growing up amid broken and unchanging souls taught me early on the importance of self-reflection. I've seen people—parents, siblings—stuck in patterns too stubborn to shift, often too late to mend the damage they left in their wake. Yet I chose a different path. I reformed my values and reshaped relationships over and over, always with the intention of improving not just myself but those around me.

I remember foolish moments with painful clarity: when Rosemary convinced me to stick my finger into a live socket, when Ken Kramer talked me into swapping shifts at the Free Press and I lost precious study time, and even the time I watched a scam unfold before my eyes, paralyzed by curiosity. And there were betrayals—a trusted friend borrowing money with a promise, only to vanish, and my brother Wally's blind faith in a dubious opportunity that dragged me into failure.

Perfection is an illusion I've come to accept. I often tell Linh, "You are the most perfect person I've ever known," a sentiment that brings a smile even as she teases me about my many shortcomings—and, admittedly, about her questionable Facebook health tips. In our shared laughter and the small victories of everyday life, I find a bittersweet tribute to the efforts we all make to find life's happiness.

Some Free Advice

Reflecting on my life, a German professor once reminded me, "Advice is free and worth every penny." Here's what I've learned over decades of missteps and moments of grace:

Plan and Adapt: Write down a vision for the next few years, but be ready to pivot when life takes an unexpected turn.

Short-Term Focus: Especially as you age, set realistic, month-by-month goals. What can you accomplish this month? Next month?

Stay True: Hold tight to your ethics and values, even when every voice around you shouts for compromise.

Keep Your Eyes Open: People aren't always what they seem. Observe their actions over time, and trust your gut.

Embrace the Journey: Appreciate what you've had and what you've lost; regret only diminishes the lessons learned.

Share, Don't Control: In relationships, give space for individual growth. Respect and love flourish when control fades.

Risk and Reward: Calculate the risk, then dare to take a chance—each risk is a lesson in itself.

Value Education: Never stop learning, and always help others rise with you.

Live Fully: When your final day comes, spend every last moment with all you've got.

In the end, life is unpredictable—a series of twists and turns that neither destiny nor perfection can fully direct. I've lived, I've learned, and now I choose to treasure every moment of this remarkable, unrepeatable journey.

ABOUT THE AUTHOR

Bob began his life's journney in Detroit Michigan, June 5, 1937, as the youngest of four children. Growing up in the 1940s and 1950s, school and family had their challenges. He worked his way through college at the Detroit Free Press advertising department, and after three years in the U.S Army teaching advanced electronics at Fort Bliss, graduated with his Bachelor of Science Degree in Electrical Engineering. His first engineering position was in New Orleans with the Saturn V space program, followed by eight years with G.E. in Cincinnati on large jet engine development. He returned to New Orleans with his wife Linda and two children, starting a global adventure that would last almost 50 years, steeped in engineering and international marketing. In his travels, he had special companions and in later years, a smiling Vietnamese lady,

Linh. From his early twenties, he followed existentialist philosophers Kafka, Sartre, and Camus with a dash of Arther Schopenhauer thrown in. They would influenced how he lived his life - always the observer, tutor, mentor and companion to all the people he touched in this experience, as he left a trail of acheivements with a few setbacks and regrets. His memory vividly recalling even events from childhood, examining details as suggested by Socrates. Life with few regrets.